—GREAT—
RUGBY MOMENTS

GREAT RUGBY MOMENTS

GARETH EDWARDS
AND ALUN WYN BEVAN

Gomer

Published in 2015 by
Gomer Press, Llandysul, Ceredigion, SA44 4JL

ISBN 978 1 78562 035 5

A CIP record for this title is available from the British Library

© text: Gareth Edwards and Alun Wyn Bevan, 2015
© photographs: as credited throughout the book
Frontispiece: *Gareth Edwards against France at Cardiff in 1976.* (Colorsport/Colin Elsey)
Pages 150–151: *Bobby Windsor looks on as Gareth Edwards tries to escape Duncan Madsen's clutches at Murrayfield in 1977.* (Colorsport/Colin Elsey)

This book is published with the financial support of the
Welsh Books Council.

The publishers would also like to acknowledge the generous contributions made by the
Press Association and Colorsport to the publication of this book.

www.paimages.co.uk   www.colorsport.co.uk

Printed and bound in Wales at
Gomer Press, Llandysul, Ceredigion

CONTENTS

CONTENTS (CONTINUED)

FOREWORD

Be careful what you wish for!

By his own admission, Gareth Edwards broke from a ruck around the side of the Welsh and Scottish forwards in the Five Nations Championship match of 1972 'just looking for a little snipe around the blind side'.

What ensued from that humble intent was for me the try that best epitomised Gareth Edwards. We can argue and debate until doomsday as to the merits of his many tries, for Wales, the Lions, Cardiff and the Barbarians. With respect, it is a fatuous exercise.

Each had its own merits, each was in a different context, at different times. Some were scored from 70 metres, some from seven. Does distance alone marginalise some, magnify others? Surely not.

But from this rugby writer's perspective, his try against Scotland that famously earned him a dousing of red shale and liquid mud, was the best of all. It was dramatic, yes, although perhaps not as dramatic as the hair-raising conclusion to the finest try ever constructed by the Barbarians. But Edwards's effort against the Scots was the epitome of everything he offered as a supreme practitioner of his sport. Firstly, the desire to probe the Scottish defence, to spy any gaps he might exploit. Edwards was a master at this trait. In a flash, he could unearth and barge through the eye of a needle.

Then there was the immense physicality and fitness, the brushing aside of Scottish back-row man Rodger Arneil as he surged clear of the forwards. This great physicality was to Edwards as the last arrow in his quiver was to the Tudor archer.

How many players of Test match quality found themselves thrust aside, hurled away by the explosive power of the Welshman's jolting hand-off? New Zealand's Bob Burgess was one memorable recipient of the thrust as he flailed unsuccessfully at the Lions scrum-half on that record-breaking 1971 tour.

Against Scotland in that single movement that led to his try, Edwards revealed more of his myriad talents. The huge strength and physicality in smashing through Arneil's attempted tackle preceded his next task: decision making. Should he attempt to kick past the covering Scotland full-back, or wait for support to arrive? And if he kicked, what type if kick was most appropriate in the conditions. Should he kick long, perhaps forcing the Scots to scramble the ball into touch near their own line? Or should he try to kick short, hoping to regather himself and continue the move?

A chip and chase in Cardiff colours, against the Harlequins in 1977. (Press Association)

In a trice, another of his great qualities emerged, quick thinking and his ability to make instant decisions. He kicked, or rather chipped the Scotland defender, only to be confounded by the bounce of the ball which refused to sit up for him.

No matter, this required yet another of Edwards's great attributes: control of the ball. Somehow, even at top speed which he needed to arrive first at the bouncing ball, he managed to put a boot on it which ensured it did not spin off sideways or cannon over the dead-ball line. The precision needed to weight that kick ahead almost to the exact position he sought to reach it before it rolled out of play was an inherent quality. You couldn't acquire that skill unless you were born with it.

Of course, two other ingredients in this pot pourri of sporting excellence were essential, like salt and pepper to the chef's skills. Courage and confidence needed to be applied liberally for it to be a success. Gareth Edwards exuded both throughout his career, as a long line of dejected, beaten opponents would testify. The physical courage he always epitomised was never better illustrated than on the Lions 1974 tour of South Africa. Hard, ferocious opponents saw him as the key cog in the Lions engine. Get to him, eliminate him and the machine would malfunction, they reasoned.

Many tried but none succeeded. Edwards took a battering at times but few handled such treatment with greater equanimity. It was the game, he argued, the essence of the sport. Just something to be accommodated, which he did time and again with aplomb.

All these factors combined in the great Welshman's remarkable try that day against Scotland at Cardiff Arms Park. Bill McLaren called it 'the sheer magic of Gareth Edwards'.

But perhaps we focus too intently on Edwards the rugby player. Should any man be known solely for his exploits in a sporting jersey? Ought not his character, make-up, humanity and consideration for fellow human beings, be the ultimate arbiter in our judgement of any man? In essence, what really maketh a man?

Just a precious few sportsmen ever manage to transcend that mythical barrier between sporting excellence and people of supreme humanity. Bobby Charlton did it in the world of football. Gareth Edwards, like Charlton now a thoroughly justified knight of the realm, has also scaled what we might term the ultimate fence of life.

On sentry duty for Wales against Ireland at a straw-strewn Arms Park in 1969.

(Colorsport/Colin Elsey)

Indeed, perhaps the greatest moments of Gareth Edwards's life have come far away from the rugby field. The manner in which he has remained humble, his courtesy in the face of all comers and his cheerful help for other people have offered young men and women of any pursuit a template as to how to live their lives.

Might not these attributes stand alongside or perhaps even surpass the greatest moments of Sir Gareth Edwards' sporting career?

Peter Bills

A Lion sizing up the Springboks at Port Elizabeth in 1974. (Colorsport/Colin Elsey)

*To begin at the beginning: the statue of
William Webb Ellis at Rugby School.*

(Press Association)

1 'MY BALL'
WILLIAM WEBB ELLIS

The Birth of Rugby Football

1823 – a pivotal year in British history? Not particularly; eight years had
passed since Wellington's victory at Waterloo and another eight would come
and go before the Merthyr Riots. However, it was in 1823 that a young lad
playing a game of, well no one is quite sure what, broke the rules and instead of
kicking the ball, had the temerity to pick it up, run with it in both hands and
apparently touch down at the far end of the field of play.

*The William Webb Ellis Trophy,
the Rugby World Cup*

(Press Association)

The young lad in question was of course William Webb Ellis and the
location of this innovative move was Rugby School, a public school halfway
between Leicester and Northampton. Little did he know at the time that he
would set in motion a process which has resulted in the game of rugby being
played on all five continents. But is this fact or fantasy?

According to school records, Rugby were playing Sedburgh (alma mater
of former England captain, Will Carling), and paintings of the period show a
cluster of boys chasing after a ball – again it is not clear if the game was a form
of football or what we in Wales know as 'cnapan'. It appears that the young
Ellis was the goalkeeper, but instead of defending his territory he picked up the
ball… and ran! The rest is history. Like his fellow players, we remain stunned:
what was he doing? Was he reprimanded? Punished, even? If so, was it the
whack of the cane? Or a hundred lines – 'I must not run with the ball' – in
Latin!

Whatever the outcome on the day, it was the beginning of a new sport.
In 1843 a rugby club was formed at Guy's Hospital in London, and others
followed suit, for example, Liverpool (1857), Blackheath (1862), Harlequins
(1866), Wasps (1867) and Oxford University (1869). The first club to be formed
in Wales was at St David's College, Lampeter, whilst the Welsh Rugby Union
was formed at the Castle Hotel, Neath in 1881.

*An official match ball even bears
the name of rugby's originator.*

(Press Association)

Rugby School was where it all began, however; it is here that the laws were
established and it was not long before a factory producing oval-shaped balls for
this new sport was opened in the town by the Gilbert company. The new game
was given the name of the local academy and 'rugby' was introduced into the
sporting vocabulary.

Ironically, cricket was William Webb Ellis's first love and he played with
some distinction for Oxford University. Having gained his degree he entered

the church and spent the last years of his life as rector at Magdalen Laver in Essex. Not much is known about this period of Ellis's life. However, a chance find by Ross McWhirter – joint compiler of *The Guinness Book of Records* and presenter of the television programme *The Record Breakers* – led to the discovery of William Webb Ellis's grave in Merton near Nice in the South of France, something which has proved a source of pride for the French Rugby Federation whose chairmen make regular pilgrimages to the site. Incidentally, Ireland claim William Webb Ellis as one of their own as he was born in Tipperary!

The border towns of Hawick and Jedburgh claim they were responsible for expanding the game in Scotland, but is Carterhaugh near Selkirk which boasts a borders tale to rival the Webb Ellis legend. In 1815 one Walter Laidlaw caught the ball and passed to one William Riddel who took off and ran flat out towards the opposition goal. Unfortunately, before he could 'score', a man on horseback appeared from nowhere and flattened poor Riddel on the spot. If only *A Question of Sport* could tell us what happened next!

England captain Will Carling caught in an Australian crush during the 1991 Rugby World Cup final at Twickenham. Carling is a former pupil at Sedburgh, the school against whom William Webb Ellis was playing when he picked up the ball and ran.

(Press Association)

2 '... AND SENT THEM HOMEWARD TAE THINK AGAIN'

The First Ever International Match

(Raeburn Place, Edinburgh, March 27, 1871)

As an international player I was lucky enough to travel widely, but my favourite away fixture was always the one against Scotland in Edinburgh.

The Friday afternoon before each match was designated an official period of 'relaxation and reflection'. How better to do this than via a leisurely stroll along Princes Street? Our hotel, the North British, was perfectly positioned to allow easy access to Jenners and Binns department stores, the Scott monument and the city gardens, not to mention the small independent stores with their typically 'Scottish' mementoes.

The Edinburgh of 1871 was a very different place, of course, but it was the home of the first ever official international match, which was played between Scotland and England at Raeburn Place. The old enemies had met twice before the previous year, at the Kennington Oval in London, but those games more resembled football than rugby as we know it today, so it was decided that a further match would be played at the beginning of the following year and 'under the rules of the parent code'. The challenge, published in *The Scotsman* and in *Bell's Life* on 8 December, 1870 read as follows:

> Almost all the leading clubs in Scotland play the Rugby code, and have no opportunity of practising the Association game even if willing to do so. We hereby challenge any team selected from the whole of England to play us a match, twenty-a-side Rugby rules either in Edinburgh or Glasgow. We can promise England a hearty welcome and a first-rate match.

Led by Frederick Stokes, the England team congregated at Euston on the Saturday evening before travelling third class on the overnight train to Waverley Station, Edinburgh, and arriving mid-morning on the Sunday. The game wasn't until the Monday afternoon and the team members had to pay all accommodation costs!

The qualifications of some of the Scottish XV were questioned in the newspapers of the day. According to John Reason and Carwyn James in *World of Rugby*, one of them was known to have travelled north across the border to shoot grouse, whilst another confessed to a liking for Scotch whisky. In

England's captain Chris Robshaw lifts the Calcutta Cup at Twickenham in 2015.

Mike Egerton/PA Wire

A Grand Slam was at stake during this Calcutta Cup match in 1990. Here Scottish try scorer Tony Stanger finds space, watched by (l. to r.) John Jeffrey, Rob Andrew, Mike Teague, Scott Hastings and Craig Chalmers. Scotland won 13–7. (Press Association)

preparation for the match, the Scottish team held a series of trial matches and were directed to keep the ball amongst the forwards. In those days to pass along the backline was seen as act of cowardice!

The England team, meanwhile, had been working on their fitness. Indeed it is said that J. H. Clayton of Liverpool would run for four miles each morning with his large Newfoundland working dog as his pacemaker, a regime supplemented by a strict diet of raw meat washed down with beer! This he did for a whole month prior to the match, so it's little wonder that England lost!

Lasting 50 minutes each way, this inaugural international could only be won by a majority of goals i.e. drop goals or converted tries (penalty goals were introduced towards the end of the century). Remarkably tries did not count as they merely enabled teams to 'try' for goal.

It was Scotland who won, by a goal and a try to a try. The winning Scottish try was hotly disputed and years later one of the Scottish umpires admitted that the decision was probably incorrect, but adding: 'I must say that when an umpire is in doubt, I think he is justified in deciding against the side which makes most noise. They are probably in the wrong.'

The honour of scoring rugby football's first international try fell to Angus Buchanan from Royal High School Former Pupils. Since 1871, various Scottish grounds have been used as international venues, including Hampden Park, Powderhall, Inverleith and the present day headquarters, Murrayfield, where I enjoyed some truly memorable scraps.

Perpetuating the oldest international rivalry of them all, Scotland's Ryan Grant tackles England's Billy Vunipola at Murrayfield in 2014. (Press Association)

3 'GO NORTH, YOUNG MAN'

The Union and League Divide

There was a time when 'Going North' was considered an act of betrayal. I knew what it was as an amateur rugby union player to be approached by ambitious rugby league clubs from the north of England, urging me to sign on the dotted line and become a professional. At the time, however, I had precious little knowledge of the history which lay behind the bitter divide between the two codes of the game.

The Northern Union (currently known as the Rugby Football League) came into being in 1895 as a result of a falling out between the northern clubs and the strictly amateur Rugby Union. The disagreement arose over payments made to players over broken time: mill workers and colliery employees in the north of England weren't being paid whilst playing rugby. This was also the case in the industrial valleys of South Wales but it was the vigorous objections and protestations of the clubs in Lancashire and Yorkshire which caused the stand off that led ultimately to a General Meeting of the Rugby Union at the Westminster Palace Hotel in London on September 20, 1893.

The northerners came in force hoping to convince the amateur body that some form of truce was required to ensure that players be allowed compensation for 'bona fide loss of time'. However, this motion was defeated by 282 votes to 136. The writing was on the wall and two years later at a highly charged assembly at the George Hotel, Huddersfield, 22 clubs (including St Helens, Leeds, Wakefield Trinity, Warrington, Widnes and Wigan) broke away fom the Rugby Union and formed the Northern Football Union. Three years later the Northern Union's brand of rugby was taken up by New Zealand and Australia. However, within a few years the 22 clubs in the Northern Union's heartland in the north of England not only reimbursed their players for losing shifts but soon embarked on the first steps of becoming fully professional.

It was the amateur rugby union code which suffered most as a result of the break up. It led to the virtual dismantling of rugby union football in Yorkshire and Lancashire whilst the divorce had a radical effect on the national side. The late 19th century had seen England, along with Scotland, dominating the international championship but following the break up England did not win another championship until 1910.

Jonathan Davies, the highest profile of all code-crossers, seen here celebrating Great Britain's win over Australia at Wembley in 1994. (Colorsport)

Robert Gate in his excellent book *Gone North – Volume 1* reminds us that the biggest migration of Welsh players to rugby league has always come in times of economic recession. So for many the exodus was an escape from poverty to guaranteed employment. I well remember the tales of chauffeured Bentleys arriving in the Amman Valley with rich club chairmen from Lancashire in their camel coats and astrakhan collars, smoking King Edward cigars, enticing talented rugby youngsters with money they could only dream of at the time. Indeed my father Glan and father-in-law Luther recollected locals like Ted Ward, Emrys Evans, Billo Rees, Dai 'Cefnder' Davies, Jac Elwyn Evans and others who decided to accept the challenge and profited from their association with the thirteen-a-side game.

John Bevan, the Wales and British Lions wing who went north in 1973 when he joined Warrington RLFC.

(Press Association)

Iestyn Harris, Wales's highest profile league-to-union convert, stepping past Italy's Mauro Bergamasco at the Stadio Flaminio in Rome in 2003. (Press Association)

Piri Weepu leads the haka ahead of the Rugby World Cup final in 2011. When the All Blacks played Wales in 1905, the Maori war dance was counteracted by the Welsh national anthem, sung for the first time at an international match. (Press Association)

4 HAKA AND 'HEN WLAD FY NHADAU'

Wales 3   New Zealand 0   **(Cardiff Arms Park, December 16, 1905)**

I never played in a Welsh team that beat the All Blacks. In fact, very few players have. But those who played in the first ever meeting between Wales and New Zealand did so much more than win a rugby match. They established the game of rugby as the national game of Wales.

That 1905 game is also part of national folklore in New Zealand, as is the tour which began on 30 July that year when the *Rimutaka* set sail from Wellington on a journey which ended 40 gruelling days later when the ship docked at Plymouth.

Apart from a two-day respite at Montevideo in Uruguay where extra supplies and more passengers were taken on, those on board had to endure everything that the full force of nature unleashed on them. This was truly an opportunity to sort out the men from the boys! Remarkably, this was not the first New Zealand team to embark on such an epic adventure. In 1888–1889 a team of Maoris had taken fourteen months to travel around the world during which time they played 107 games. However, this tour of 1905 is recognised as the first official visit by a team from the land of the long white cloud.

Thirty-six games had been arranged for the visitors starting with an encounter in Exeter against the English champions, Devon. The press predicted an easy win for the home team. After all, the tourists had endured a long journey and were short on practice and experience. What do the press know? The All Blacks swept to a 55–4 victory, spearheaded by their inspirational captain, Dave Gallaher. He made such an impression that one Devon committee member described him as 'a sort of blooming hermaphrodite; forward and half-back too!'

During a packed schedule which lasted three-and-a-half months, the visitors played matches in Engand, Scotland and Ireland and arrived in Cardiff on December 14 boasting some pretty impressive statistics. They played 27 matches, winning each one, scoring 801 points and yielding a miserly 22. In addition to winning each game, the manner in which the team played drew plaudits from all quarters – this was a formidable group of players, strong and fast and well organised. When Dave Gallaher and his men arrived at Cardiff Central Station they immediately became aware of the passion the Welsh public had for the oval ball game – they were surrounded by enthusiastic

Don't look now! New Zealand's Mils Muliaina 1s sandwiched between Shane Williams and Mark Taylor (right) at the 2003 Rugby World Cup.

(Press Association)

Gwyn Nicholls, Wales's victorious captain in 1905.

(Press Association)

The menacing and inspirational Dave Gallaher.

(Press Association)

fans whose welcome was genuine and sincere. It took the charabancs an hour to travel a distance of a quarter of a mile to their hotel in Westgate Street. They were also aware that Wales hadn't lost a home game since 1899 with the Welsh press keen to remind them that Wales were the current Triple Crown holders.

The Welsh Rugby Union and its secretary, Walter Rees, had been preparing meticulously for the big match. To counteract the effects of the Maori War Dance they granted permission for the players to sing the National Anthem, a song composed in 1856 by the Pontypridd weaver-publicans Evan and John James. The press, in the weeks leading up to the match, described the clash as 'a world championship encounter'. There was widespread interest with 50 trains arriving in Cardiff from all over Wales as well as the Midlands, Lancashire and London. Prominent businessmen agreed to close Cardiff Docks early so as to allow their workers to make their way to the Arms Park whilst restaurants stocked up on food. The main gates were opened at 12 noon with ticket booths making a roaring trade right up to kick-off. The atmosphere was electric with vendors selling everything from rosettes to hot chestnuts. Spectators started arriving hours before kick-off and were entertained by the Welsh Regiment's 2nd Battalion Band.

Preparation for the match had been methodical with players and administrators leaving no stone unturned. Although the selected XV included several academics, the task of preparing the team was left to Dickie Owen, the boilermaker from the Hafod area of Swansea. It was the diminutive scrum-half who assumed the role of coach when the team assembled some 24 hours prior to kick-off; he dictated the tactics and ensured that all team members were comfortable with various combinations and ploys.

Dave Gallaher and his fellow players were well aware that this was to be their hardest contest to date. They knew all about Percy Bush from the Lions tour to New Zealand in 1904 where he had been a devastating runner. For the first time in the history of rugby union both teams ran onto the field wearing numbered jerseys; the dye was cast when both teams made telling statements prior to kick-off – the crowd stood in silence for the Haka whilst the Welshmen responded with a lung-bursting rendition of 'Hen Wlad Fy Nhadau'.

No quarter was asked or given during the first few minutes with both captains, Gwyn Nicholls and Dave Gallaher, determined to inspire their respective teams to victory. Wales nearly scored when

Willie Llewellyn held on to a difficult pass behind his back but unfortunately lost possession in an attempt to get to the line. New Zealand had difficulty in mounting any serious attacks as a result of an effective Welsh defence whilst the all-conquering All Blacks surprisingly found the Welsh forwards difficult to overcome. And then after 23 minutes play Wales took the lead with a try orchestrated by Dickie Owen. At a scrummage some 20 yards from the near touchline, and 30 yards from the New Zealand goal-line (Westgate Street end) Owen called the move. Bush, Nicholls and Llewellyn lined up menacingly on the blind side and attracted the attention of the All Blacks. Owen secured a quick heel and darted towards the touchline. Then in a flash he stopped in his tracks throwing a long pass in the other direction to Cliff Pritchard who was the extra back in the Welsh line-up, monitoring every move made by the menacing Dave Gallaher. The All Blacks had been temporarily wrong footed. Pritchard, taking the ball off his toes, found Rhys Gabe in support who instinctively handed on to the supporting Teddy Morgan who sprinted 20 yards to score in the corner! It was a never-to-be-forgotten moment in Welsh rugby history.

New Zealand will claim that Bob Deans was denied an equalising try by the referee John Dallas but the record books will forever read: Wales 3 New Zealand 0. After the game Gallaher paid tribute to Wales's performance: 'It was a rattling good game, played out to the bitter end. The better team won.'

Cardiff has been a happy hunting ground for New Zealand since 1905, where they have lost only twice to Wales. Here winning All Blacks captain Graham Mourie dives over to seal victory in 1980, as Terry Holmes arrives too late.

(Colorsport)

9, 10, Black: John Gallagher takes on Welsh half-backs Robert Jones
(9) and Jonathan Davies in the semi-final of the inaugural Rugby
World Cup in 1987. There was to be none of the controversy of
1905, however, as the All Blacks ran out 49–6 winners.

(Colorsport/Colin Elsey)

Fifty years after my first visit to Twickenham, Leigh Halfpenny (15) and Owen Farrell do balletic aerial battle as Wales lose to England in 2014.

(Colorsport)

5 CABBAGE PATCH KIDS

The Consecration of Twickenham

John Reason, doyen of rugby writers, once described Twickenham, like Lord's and Wimbledon, as an institution, and as one who played there on numerous occasions I have to agree.

Jean Denis, who in the 1970s contributed regular articles to the French newspaper *Sud-Ouest*, describes the stadium as 'the cathedral of rugby football'. Some might have preferred the Arms Park, Eden Park or Ellis Park, but, to many, it is Twickenham which has the aura which makes it one of sport's truly great venues.

The Rugby Union, back in the first decade of the 20th century, heeded the advice of Billy Williams, former player and referee, and purchased approximately 11 acres of market garden at Twickenham for the princely sum of £5572 12s 6d. Previously, England had travelled the length and breadth of the country and played international matches in London (Kennington Oval, Blackheath, the Crystal Palace, and Richmond) as well as further afield in Manchester, Leeds, Dewsbury, Leicester, Bristol and Gloucester.

The first ever game played on the ground (affectionately known as 'the Cabbage Patch') was on October 2, 1909 when Harlequins entertained Richmond and in front of 2,000 spectators beat them 14–10. On January 15, 1910 England defeated Wales 11–6 in the first international match played on the hallowed turf; England hadn't beaten Wales for 11 years and many believed that the spell would never be broken!

The match is best remembered for a quite remarkable score in the first minute of play. Ben Gronow kicked off for Wales towards the South End and when Adrian Stoop took possession everyone present waited for the customary kick to touch. But Stoop's philosophy was based on attack. He veered to the right before changing direction to run upfield. Although eventually boxed in, he put in a deft punt which panicked the Welsh defence. England's chase was a good one. They regained possession and via Louis Birkett got the ball out to Fred Chapman of West Hartlepool who was over the try line without a hand being laid on him. Hundreds of spectators in the process of getting to their seats missed out on the drama of a score from which Wales were never able to recover. Astonishingly, Wales would have to wait another 23 years before winning their first international at the ground.

New Zealand's Colin Meads wins a lineout during my first big match at Twickenham, as the Barbarians lose 11–6 in 1967.

(Press Association)

I well remember my first visit to Twickenham back in 1964, when my sister Gloria and her husband Clive took me to see Wales playing England. For a 16-year-old lad from Gwaun-cae-gurwen, the sight of the towering grand stands and of the masses milling around was enough to get the pulse racing – not to mention line upon line of limousines, from which high-class hampers emerged. I can still picture those popping champagne corks!

When we eventually made it to our seats, the noise from the 83,000 strong crowd was something else. I'm sure it was just the three of us shouting for Wales! The match ended in a 6–6 draw, John Ranson and David Perry's tries for England being matched by Dewi Bebb's brace for Wales. Wales actually had a golden opportunity to win the match in the closing minutes but Grahame Hodgson's straightforward penalty attempt sailed wide.

Three years later I was privileged to run onto the field in Barbarian colours in a memorable encounter against the All Blacks. We deserved to win but two match-saving tackles by Fergie McCormick spared their blushes. The following year I scored my first international try for Wales on the ground with both teams again sharing the spoils.

As a former player I can truly testify to Twickenham's charm. It's no wonder that we continue, like Max Boyce, to 'pay our weekly shilling for that January trip'!

Two-try hero Dewi Bebb about to take Keith Bradshaw's pass at Twickenham in 1964. If you look carefully, you might be able to spot me cheering Wales on in the crowd…

(Press Association)

6 A REAL ALLROUNDER

Eric Liddell, Stade Colombes 1922 and 1924

Most of the great moments listed in this book have been the products of spontaneity. What is more, their impact was felt as soon as they had been enacted. Others, however, may have been of no consequence initially: it is only subsequently that their signifcance has become apparent, and even then possibly for personal reasons only.

Take the great Scottish athlete Eric Liddell, for instance, whose moving tale was told in the 1981 film *Chariots of Fire*. He was one of the favourites to win the 100 metres at the Paris Olympics in 1924 but his Christian convictions prevented him from taking part because the heats were to be held on a Sunday. Remarkably, however, an eleventh-hour invitation to run in the 400 metres (an event in which he had never previously competed) resulted in his winning the gold medal.

Liddell had featured on the wing for Edinburgh University's first XV where his partnership with Leslie Gracie soon came to the attention of the national selectors. It was no surprise therefore when the call came to play for Scotland, at the start of the 1922–23 season, against France at Stade Colombes in Paris. This is where I, too, would make my international debut in April 1967.

Eric Liddell played for Scotland on seven occasions, scoring three tries including a fine individual effort against Wales at Cardiff Arms Park in February 1923. At the end of the season he was advised to concentrate on his athletics career in preparation for the 1924 Olympic Games. His final match for Scotland was in the 1923 Calcutta Cup match at Inverleith, a match England won by the narrowest of margins.

How good was he as a rugby player? With no video evidence and no one to speak on his behalf, one must trust in newspaper reports of the period, including the following piece which appeared in *The Scotsman* prior to his international selection:

His great speed is not his only asset; for not only did he 'round' one and sometimes two opponents when he scored, but time and again he had to use both resource and initiative. Never once was he found wanting. He showed an almost uncanny intuition for being in the right place at the right time.

Scotland's Eric Liddell, a genuine allrounder. (Press Association)

'I have finished the race, I have kept the faith...' Eric Liddell (left) wins 400-metre Olympic gold at Stade Colombes in 1924.

(Press Association)

And it was *The Scotsman*, too, which had this to say after Liddell's international debut:

> The Gracie-Liddell wing was as meteoric and mercurial as ever; Liddell was the more efficent of the two, and seemed to be putting more fire in his play than is his wont.

As someone who has dabbled in several disciplines over the years, I am full of admiration for those who have succeeded in more than one sport. Liddell did it in the 1920s; Maurice Turnbull played at scrum-half in Wales's first ever victory at Twickenham in 1933 and also played cricket for Glamorgan and England in the early 1930s. Ken Jones won 44 caps for Wales and picked up a silver medal in Britain's 4x100m relay team in London's 1948 Olympics. Across the Atlantic Jim Thorpe won a gold medal at the Stockholm Olympics in 1912 and then went on to win huge accolades at American Football, baseball and basketball.

Over the last few years, such sportsmen have become few and far between as athletes are encouraged to concentrate on their specialist discipline. An exception in the professional-rugby era was Jeff Wilson who won 60 caps for the All Blacks and then played a one-day series for the cricketing Black Caps.

I once had aspirations as a sporting allrounder, but I now know that the only thing Eric Liddell and I truly have in common is that we both won our first caps in Paris!

All Black and Black Cap Jeff Wilson on the charge against Australia in 1998.

(Press Association)

7 THE FLYING SCOTSMAN ON THE MUMBLES ROAD

Ian Smith, Full Steam Ahead   (Barbarians v Swansea, St Helen's, April 21, 1924)

I can only marvel at his achievements. Statistically his records are extraordinary – he scored 11 tries in his first five matches for Scotland!

Ian Scott Smith is still Scotland's top try scorer (he shares the record with Tony Stanger); a remarkable feat considering the number of games played by our current crop of international rugby players. Born in Australia to Scottish parents, he was brought up in New Zealand and educated at Winchester College and Oxford University before finishing his studies in Scotland, the country he always considered home. Yes, he was qualified to play for several countries, but his commitment to Scotland was never in doubt and he went on to represent the dark blues on 32 occasions scoring 24 tries, an impressive strike rate in any era. This total remained an international record until it was eventually broken by David Campese in 1987 and remained a Five/Six Nations record until surpassed by Brian O'Driscoll in 2011.

Wales's Rowe Harding, Smith's team-mate with the 1924 British Lions in South Africa, reckoned him the greatest wing of all time. Unfortunately, action replays, zooms and slowmos weren't available in Ian Smith's days and as a result we are totally dependent on newspaper reports and hand-me-down descriptions of electrifying performances by heroic figures of the time. Ian Smith was one such figure and was accorded god-like status in Scotland and beyond.

Smith was nicknamed 'the Flying Scotsman' and one of his most memorable tries was in Barbarian colours against Swansea at St Helen's on Easter Monday 1924. In his book *Fifty Two Famous Tries* my great friend J.B.G. Thomas, former sports editor and chief rugby correspondent of the *Western Mail*, recalls a conversation with Jock Wemyss who played in the match:

> The try started in the most unusual fashion when Parker's penalty kick dropped just wide of the right hand post. In true Barbarian fashion we decided to counter-attack with George Aitken sending the ball out to Arthur Wallace taking the ball a mere ten yards from our try-line. Arthur drew his man releasing Ian Smith who took up the challenge racing for the Mumbles Road end 85 yards away. Harding gave chase with the Flying Scotsman enjoying a three-yard lead. At that time Smith

The statistically extraordinary Ian Smith.   (Press Association)

and Harding were two of the fastest men in European rugby and although Harding gained a yard or so he was never near enough to effect a diving tackle. At the halfway line the Swansea full-back Phil Lloyd came across to launch a desperate diving tackle on Smith. However, Ian Smith in full cry leaned inwards and moved in a fine arc to touch down behind the posts. The crowd, already on their feet, yelled excitedly for this had been a magnificent example of Barbarian football. I took the conversion and missed! Swansea 11 Barbarians 9. I must have been dazzled by the magnificence of Smith's wonderful try!

Rowe Harding, the Welsh international wing who couldn't catch the Flying Scotsman at Swansea!

Ireland's Brian O'Driscoll, breaker of Ian Smith's great record, is seen here rounding Italy's Fabio Ongaro to score yet another Six Nations try in Dublin in 2004.

8 SWEEPING THEM OFF THEIR FEET

George Nepia   **(St Helen's, Swansea, November 29, 1924)**

The All Blacks have always been blessed with brilliant full-backs, from Billy Wallace, George Nepia, Bob Scott, Don Clarke, John Gallagher, Christian Cullen to their current superstar, Israel Dagg. But, according to Bob Howitt and Dianne Howarth in *All Black Magic*, if they were to be measured purely in terms of their defensive attributes, one of them would tower over the rest. George Nepia came to prominence during New Zealand's tour of Britain and France in 1924–25 where Cliff Porter's men played a total of 30 games, winning every single one. Only 19 years of age, Nepia played every single match on tour, but one of his finest moments came against Wales at St Helen's in Swansea. F.J. Ohlson, headmaster of Maungawhau School, who toured with the team, takes up the story in his column in *The Evening Post*:

The peerless George Nepia.

> The most wonderful feat of defence by attack I ever saw was brought off by George Nepia. Three Welshmen had broken through and were coming down our lines with only Nepia to stop them. It looked like a moral try, but Nepia suddenly made a leaping rush and dive for the ball, throwing himself right into the three attackers, who were bunched, and swept them all off their feet. He got the ball and cleared.

New Zealand won 19–0 with George Nepia receiving the plaudits, including this splendid report in the *Western Mail*: 'There were times when it appeared that nothing would stay the fierce rushes of the Welsh pack. By sheer strength they barged their way through with the ball and there stood Nepia alone between them and their desired objective… His judgement is uncanny and his pluck magnificent… Nepia was a stone wall which the Welshmen hurled against in vain.'

There is no doubt that Nepia was out of the ordinary. He was never afraid to come upfield and join the line with confidence, for he had learned the game as a five eighth. He preferred to run at opponents, who had to absorb the full shock of his 13 stones of bone and muscle to halt him. But he was also adept at all the other things at which full-backs must be expert – safe catching, accurate kicking and brutally hard tackling. He had no peer.

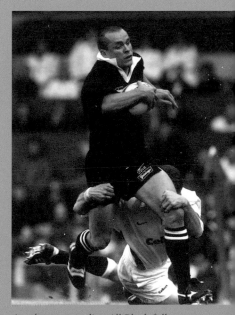

Another outstanding All Black full-back, Christian Cullen, scorer of 46 tries in 58 Tests between 1996–2003.

Indeed, as Denzil Batchelor wrote in *The Times*, 'It is not for me a question of whether Nepia was the best full-back in history. It is a question of which of the others is fit to loose the laces of his Cotton Oxford boots'.

A sad post-script is that in 1927 George Nepia was on stand-by for New Zealand's first-ever tour of South Africa. However, at the last minute he was told that he would not be eligible to visit the Republic. Alas, the rumblings of apartheid were already beginning to be heard.

Choke and Dagger! The latest inheritor of George Nepia's jersey and mantle, Israel Dagg, squeezes between two Aussies in Brisbane in 2014. (Press Association)

9 SLOW TOO QUICK FOR SPRINGBOKS!

Leicestershire and East Midlands 30   South Africa 21

(Leicester, November 14, 1931)

Never understimate the invitational team, but when the South African tourists of 1931–32 came to Leicester undefeated, they were more than quietly confident of victory.

Their style of play throughout the four-month tour had caused controversy! They either kicked directly to touch to gain territory or diagonally across the field to create possible opportunities for the wing three-quarters. It was not attractive but mightily effective. The Welsh journalist 'Old Stager' was not amused: 'The Africans by adhering to ten man rugby are winning their matches but are not capturing the hearts and minds of rugby followers'.

However, the scoreline at Leicester that day was extraordinary. Howard Marshall in the Monday edition of *The Daily Telegraph* stated categorically that the combined team trounced the Springboks fairly and squarely by six goals (one dropped, one penalty) and a try to two goals (one dropped) and four tries.

For the first time on tour the South African management decided to rest their captain and kicker Bennie Osler. In a ten-try epic it was ironic, therefore, that the men from the Midlands should win by dint of their goal-kicking. Springbok supporters were quick to maintain that they would not have lost if Osler had played; then again, they would not have scored five tries if he had! Replacement stand-off Micky Francis opted for an attractive 15-man game which resulted in wing Morris Zimmerman crossing for four tries.

At Leicester the match was superbly controlled by Charles Slow of Northampton, a largely unknown stand-off who won just a solitary cap for England when they defeated Scotland in 1934 to win the Triple Crown. He was killed in a motor accident while serving with the RAF Volunteer Reserve in April 1939. Against the Springboks Snow scored two tries and dropped a goal. Irish international George Beamish, along with Hardwick and Buckingham, scored the other tries, with Weston converting four.

Never before had a touring team had so many points scored against them. Apparently, according to John Billot in his book *Springboks in Wales*, the South Africans had sung merrily in their coach on their way from London but ever since singing has been taboo for the Springbok team before matches. It was the day when the South Africans scored five tries – and lost!

Skipper and kicker Bennie Osler, in the stand when his Springboks lost at Leicester.   (Press Association)

George Beamish, try scorer at Leicester.   (Press Association)

10 THE ALL WHITES BEAT THE ALL BLACKS

Swansea 11 New Zealand 3   (St Helen's, Swansea, September 28, 1935)

The comics I read as a kid were full of unlikely heroics. And that's why I read them!

But who would have thought that the arrival of Jack Manchester's Third All Blacks in Swansea would herald the stuff of schoolboy dreams? With several key players injured in the 3–0 defeat to Cardiff the previous Saturday, the selectors had had to resort to recalling former players to help them out in a crisis. Full-back Edryd Jones had been borrowed from the Metropolitan Police and Claude Davey drafted into the centre, thanks to a positive reply from Sale RFC.

However, the news that two Gowerton Grammar School sixth-formers had been included in the All Whites line-up divided supporters into two camps. Whilst some applauded the selectors' vision in calling on the services of cousins Haydn Tanner and Willie Davies, others saw this as madness. It was one thing to do well on a school playing field, quite another to perform well against the best rugby team in the world!

Thus, on a wet and windy afternoon in front of a crowd of 40,000 partisan supporters, entertained pre-match by the Llansamlet Silver Band, the young and inexperienced All Whites took to the field to face the might of New Zealand, as the Christians had once been fed to the lions of the Colosseum! Indeed, as one newspaper had it, Swansea were little better than 'Lambs to the Slaughter'.

It soon became evident, however, that the Swansea forwards were able to hold their own against their much heavier opposition, allowing Tanner and Davies to dictate the course of the game. After 25 minutes play, the Swansea eight chased the ball downfield towards the Mumbles end for Dennis Hunt to claim an unconverted try. The crowd went mad.

With the Swansea pack now in full cry, a second try was on the cards. Willie Davies made a glorious break, ghosting through the defence, beating three men with ease. Claude Davey was in support and the Welsh international captain raced through to score, just as he would later again after another run by Davies.

The post-match quote from the New Zealand captain is still music to the ears: 'Please don't tell them back home that we were beaten by a pair of schoolboys!'

Haydn Tanner, Swansea and Wales, troubles the Kiwis at St Helen's in 1945. Ten years earlier, he had been one of the schoolboys who humbled Jack Manchester's tourists.

(Press Association)

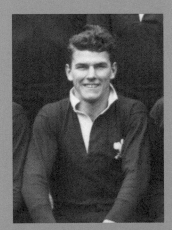

Answering Swansea's SOS, Welsh international Claude Davey scored twice on that famous day.

(Press Association)

11 THE RUSSIAN PRINCE OF GWAUN-CAE-GURWEN

Obolensky's Magic Moment   **(Twickenham, January 4, 1936)**

Some of you older readers will remember it well. In the 1950s and 1960s news bulletins weren't only confined to radio and television broadcasts. We were regularly updated on events the world over during our weekly visits to the cinema where Movietone and Pathe News provided valuable up-to-date information prior to the main film.

It must have been 1960, a quarter of a century after England beat New Zealand at Twickenham for the first time, that I first saw the exotically-named winger score the try which won that very game. It is still etched in my memory. Though the footage was grainy, the stained images of Obolensky straining nerve and sinew resulted in a huge roar in Gwaun-cae-gurwen's Workingmen's Hall.

Alexander Obolensky, born in Petrograd in 1916, was a Russian prince and an officer of the Imperial Horse Guards who was brought to England to escape the Russian Revolution in 1917, and his try was one of the most talked about sporting moments of the 1930s.

In fact Obolensky crossed for two tries during England's 13–0 victory, the first a mere sprint along the right-hand touchline, whilst the second was simply inspirational. Cranmer and Candler had set up the opportunity with an attack on the right. Their intention was to create space for Obolensky but the raw 20-year-old supplied a touch of unorthodoxy which baffled the opposition and his own team-mates. He checked in full stride, wrong footed the defence by veering left and eventually opened up a long diagonal gap. On he went with Mitchell in pusuit, but Obolensky was in full flight. He lengthened his stride further and miraculously got to the line in front of a bewildered defence.

Sadly, in March 1940, Alexander Obolensky was killed when his Hawker Hurricane crashed on landing at an East Anglian airfield. He was the first international player to lose his life in the Second World War.

Prince Alexander Obolensky, a name to conjure with.

(Press Association)

Bernard Gadney, captain of England the day Obolensky's tries sank New Zealand.

(Press Association)

Twickenham continues to relish the visit of the All Blacks, where England have beaten New Zealand on five occasions. But not in 2014 when Richie McCaw scored this try, in spite of Dylan Hartley's best efforts.

(Press Association)

12 'Skrum, Skrum, Skrum'

New Zealand 6   South Africa 17   (Eden Park, Auckland, September 25, 1937)

Dr Danie Craven, seen here as coach of the 1952 Sprinboks, knew how to beat the All Blacks in 1937.

(Press Association)

You don't win a Test series against New Zealand in their own back yard without being a bit special. The 1971 Lions managed it, but, surprisingly, only one South African team has managed it.

The 1937 Springboks, led by Philip Nel, were considered the finest team to represent South Africa prior to the Second World War. During their three-month tour of Australia and New Zealand their forwards impressed their hosts with the strength of their scrummaging, their defensive qualities and all-round aggression. With such a solid platform their half-backs could dictate play and it was no surprise when they eventually clinched the series.

The All Blacks won the first Test at Wellington but it could be argued that there were extenuating circumstances. Mystifyingly, the inspirational Nel was left out of the Springboks' starting line-up, whilst Boy Louw and Gerry Brand (two consistently vital sparks to the team's spirit) were injured. What is more, for some inexplicable reason, scrum-half Danie Craven was selected at outside half.

The visitors were at full strength for the second Test at Christchurch, however, and deservedly won 13–6. It was a combination of High Noon and Gunfight at the OK Kraal for the series decider at Eden Park – the All Blacks had never lost a Test series at home and the Springboks had not lost a series since 1896. It was billed as a world-title contest with tickets at a premium. A record crowd of 60,000 packed the stadium.

Before kick-off a telegram was read out in the South African dressing room; it was from Paul Roos, the Springboks' captain during their 1906 tour of the United Kingdom. It simply read, 'Skrum, skrum, skrum'.

Nel took heed, opting for scrummages rather than lineouts throughout. The home side just couldn't compete with their powerful opponents and were constantly on the back foot, surrendering territory and possession. It was all rather embarrassing. With the forwards dominating all phases of play and Danie Craven, restored to his usual position, playing a vital role with stand-off partner Tony Harris, the All Blacks were beaten in all departments. It was a 15-man performance which saw three-quarters Dai Owen Williams, Fred Turner and Louis Babrow claiming four of the five tries.

Paul Roos, captain of the 1906 Sprinboks, and sender of the straight-talking telegram!

(Press Association)

13 DOCTOR DO-IT-ALL

Jackie Kyle and the 1948 Grand Slam

If ever I had to draw up a list of role models for my grandchildren then Jackie Kyle would be near the top of that list. I had the honour of meeting him on several occasions and remember that from our first encounter he was one of those individuals you felt comfortable with; as if I had known him all my life.

In a strange way I did feel as if I'd grown up with Jackie Kyle, for his was one of the names that constantly cropped up on the radio during rugby international weekends. In those days, before the advent of television in every sitting room, our heroes in Gwaun-cae-gurwen were those who played for Cwmgors or Swansea. But thanks to the commentaries of G.V. Wynne-Jones, Rex Alston and Peter West, we were able to follow the careers of Cliff Morgan, Peter Jackson, Jeff Butterfield, Arthur Smith, Gordon Waddell, Tony O'Reilly and the inimitable Jackie Kyle.

Doctor Jack, as he was fondly known, was the star of Irish rugby during the 1940s and 1950s. He won 46 caps over a career which spanned twelve seasons. He was an outstanding outside half, quick off the mark, an accurate kicker and extremely skilful with ball in hand. Kyle was the catalyst in Ireland's historic win at Ravenhill, Belfast in 1948.

In the days leading up to the match, the press had been rather critical of the home team's tactics and their over-reliance on the kicking game. The all-important Grand Slam match followed the same pattern but the tactic worked in Ireland's favour early in the second half when Jack Daly, who would later join Huddersfield Rugby League Football Club, chased a kick through from a lineout to score the crucial try. It was that never-to-be-forgotten moment in Irish rugby history – the crowd tore his jersey to shreds at the final whistle. Daly was carried shoulder high from the field of play but it was Jackie Kyle who had masterminded Ireland's first ever Grand Slam and their first Triple Crown since 1899.

I often heard my great friends Bleddyn Williams and Jack Matthews reminiscing about the gifted Irishman – how defenders would try to collar him only to find themselves clutching thin air! The story they most liked to recount was of the try he scored against Wales at the Arms Park in 1951. In a prepared move Kyle skipped around centre Ronnie Chambers and, as Jack Matthews closed in to tackle him, he sidestepped out of trouble, ran past Gerwyn Williams and then outsprinted Cliff Morgan to the try line. With the score tied

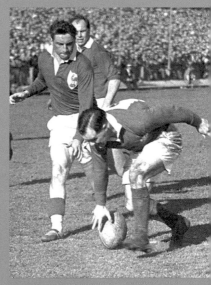

Cardiff and Wales's Jack Matthews knew at first hand how good his fellow doctor was.

(Press Association)

at 3–3 it looked as if Ken Jones would score the winning try for Wales, but he was brought down inches from the line by a quite amazing last-ditch tackle – by Jackie Kyle!

If he was a superstar on the rugby field, off it Doctor Jack was the most modest, unassuming gentleman you could ever wish to meet. It was with a great deal of sadness that I learned of his death in 2014 but his memory is still revered in the United Kingdom and Ireland, but also in Sumatra, Indonesia and Zambia where he spent some 40 years as a surgeon and missionary. A truly great man.

Karl Mullen of Old Belvedere, Ireland's Grand Slam captain in 1948. (Press Association)

Ireland's Jack Kyle, modest superstar and 1948 Grand Slam architect, takes on Dickie Jeeps (left) and Jeff Butterfield at Twickenham in 1957.

(Press Association)

14 KEEPING UP WITH THE JONESES

Three Top Tries during Four Top Years (1950–53)

Historically, Wales has always produced players who can, with a moment of magic, change the course of a game. They can be anonymous for 79 minutes, but then, like Lionel Messi, they strike, decisively and gloriously. Two such were the Jones boys, Lewis and Ken.

In 1950, at the tender age of 18 years and nine months, Lewis Jones was picked to play against England at Twickenham on January 21. Now, Wales's record at HQ was not good at the time (one win in 40 years) and perhaps this was neither the time nor the place to introduce an unproven youngster to the cauldron of international rugby. While the teams lined up for the anthems, the Welsh captain John Gwilliam could be seen whispering some words of encouragement in the young man's ear. This would be a baptism of fire!

The Welsh team which defeated England on Lewis Jones's debut at Twickenham in Grand Slam year 1950. Captain John Gwilliam would also lead Wales to Grand Slam glory two years later.
Back row (left to right):
N.H Lambert (referee),
John Robins, Ray Cale, Bob Evans,
Roy John, Don Hayward,
Rex Willis, Lewis Jones.
Centre row, left to right:
Dai Davies, Cliff Davies,
Jack Matthews, John Gwilliam,
Billy Cleaver, Ken Jones.
Seated, left to right:
Trevor Brewer, Malcolm Thomas.

(Press Association)

'All yours, Rex!' Newport's Ken Jones passes the ball out to Cardiff scrum-half Rex Willis during another Welsh victory at Twickenham, this time in 1952.

Press Association)

Ken Jones sprints for the line with Olympic efficiency against France in 1950.

(Press Association)

England were the first to score when, after eight minutes, John Smith intercepted a wayward pass and ran 40 yards to the line. However, just before half-time, a kick from England full-back Murray Hofmeyr dropped short of the halfway line. Lewis Jones was supposed to gather and kick the ball safely into touch but to everybody's amazement the young full-back set off on a run which resulted in one of the most talked-about tries of the post-war period.

After gathering the ball, Jones realised that the pedestrian England defence wouldn't prevent him crossing the advantage line and soon he found himself in acres of space. With the Twickenham crowd on its feet in anticipation, he fooled the opposition with two outrageous dummies before he was finally brought to ground. However, Jones had already handed on to the supporting Malcolm Thomas who had Bob Evans and subsequently Cliff Davies in support. It was the Kenfig Hill and Cardiff front-row forward who eventually crossed the line for a try which secured a 11–5 win and led eventually to a Grand Slam.

Six months later, Lewis Jones found himself on a flight to New Zealand having been invited to join the British Lions touring party to replace the injured Irishman George Norton. Lewis certainly took full advantage of his opportunity and produced an outstanding performance for the tourists at Eden Park, Auckland in the final Test match of the series on June 29.

Although the Lions lost 11–8, Lewis created a try which the *New Zealand Weekly News* rugby reporter described as 'the finest of the century'. At a Lions defensive scrummage and with the All Blacks positioned for the inevitable kick into touch, the Lions decided to run the ball from behind their own goal line. Outside half Jackie Kyle threw a rushed pass to Bleddyn Williams but the ball did not reach him as Lewis Jones had appeared from nowhere between them and was now dancing his way through the oppostion and racing towards the halfway line. A quick glance to the right confirmed that the ever-reliable Ken Jones was at his shoulder and as he came head to head with Bob Scott he presented the wing three-quarter with a perfect pass, allowing the Olympic sprinter a clear run-in for the line. Awesome!

Ken Jones knew a thing or two about memorable tries… December 19, 1953, and it was all-square in the Wales-New Zealand match with barely five minutes remaining on the referee's watch when a moment of inspiraton from open-side wing forward Clem Thomas resulted in heartache for Bob Stuart's XV. On New Zealand's 10-yard line on the South Stand side near the touchline an Allan Elsom error gifted the ball to Thomas who decided on a speculative cross-kick. The ball bounced, and in so doing wrong footed All Black wing three-quarter Ron Jarden, allowing Ken Jones to gather and glide towards the posts on the River Taff side for the winning try. Had the bounce been kinder to Jarden, it could well have resulted in an All Blacks victory. It finished 13–8, putting Wales ahead 3–1 ahead in the matches played between these two great countries. It remains to this very day the last time for Wales to defeat New Zealand in a Test match.

Bob Scott, New Zealand full-back when Ken Jones's try helped Wales beat the 1953 All Blacks. These Kiwis are so tough they don't even need boots! (Press Association)

To the Victor the spoils… Victor Matfield wins clean lineout ball in spite of Jamie Heaslip's stretch during the latest incarnation of Lions v Springboks spectaculars, the third test at Ellis Park, Johannesburg in 2009. The tableau is completed by (from the left) Martyn Williams, Jon Smit, Joe Worsley, Ryan Kankowski and Phil Vickery. Though the Lions won 28–9, they lost the series 2–1

(Press Association)

15 MORGAN THE MAGNIFICENT

South Africa 22 British Lions 23   (Ellis Park, Johannesburg, August 6, 1955)

'Some people are on the pitch… they think it's all over… it is now!' They were the immortal words uttered on commentary by Kenneth Wolstenholme when Geoff Hurst broke away and claimed his hat-trick and ultimate victory for England against West Germany in the 1966 World Cup Final at Wembley.

Similarly, Cliff Morgan produced timeless words during the Barbarians versus All Blacks match at Cardiff in 1973. 'This is great stuff… Phil Bennett covering, chased by Alistair Scown… Brilliant, oh! that's brilliant… John Williams, Bryan Williams… Pullin, John Dawes… Great dummy… David, Tom David… The half-way line: brilliant by Quinnell… This is Gareth Edwards… A dramatic start. What a score!'

My great friend Cliff Morgan was one of the most delightful and likeable individuals I've ever met. He was a man of many parts and upon

Charge! British Lions Bryn Meredith (left) and R.H. Williams close in on South Africa's Tommy Gentles during the Lions' famous victory, orchestrated by Cliff Morgan, at Ellis Park in 1955.

(Press Association)

Cliff Morgan, 'simply sensational' in South Africa in 1955. (Press Association)

Jack Siggins, Lions tour manager in 1955, seen here in Ireland colours against England in 1933. (Press Association)

retirement became the presenter of one of my favourite television programmes, *Welsh Sports Parade*. He was equally adept on radio and television and eventually graduated to one of the plum jobs in sports broadcasting namely head of the BBC's outside broadcast department. During his youth he sang in choirs, played the piano and in social gatherings was the life and soul of the party. He was also an outstanding outside half who represented Cardiff, Bective Rangers, the Barbarians, Wales, and the British Lions.

Clifford Isaac Morgan from the village of Trebanog in the Rhondda is universally recognized as one of the greatest Welsh outside halves ever. His accomplishments at club and international level made him a sporting superstar. To this very day they still sing his praises in South Africa where his performances for the British Lions in the 1955 series were simply sensational. His blistering runs on the veldt's rock-hard surfaces caused constant problems for a stretched Springboks defence with Jeff Butterfield, W.P.C. Davies and the 19-year-old Tony O'Reilly benefiting from his control and vision. I became aware of Cliff's genius when I visited South Africa with Cardiff in 1967 and the British Lions in 1968 where tales of Cliff's daring deeds remained part of folklore.

In sport, as in life, we all have our bad days. Cliff Morgan had his bad day at the Arms Park in 1951 against South Africa. He was hounded throughout by the Springbok back-row forward Basil van Wyk and readily admitted that his performance had left a lot to be desired, even blaming himself for Wales's defeat. Fast forward to 1955 and with single-minded determination Cliff decided that the first Test at Ellis Park would provide the ideal opportunity for him to erase that memory and contribute to a Lions victory. This he did with a vengeance. Cliff's try that day is an image which will forever be etched in my memory. Again I have to thank Pathe News for showing the highlights at my local cinema.

In his book *Lions Rampant*, Vivian Jenkins pays glowing tribute to Cliff's contribution, '…What followed after the interval raised the game to an altogether transcendent plane. It was Morgan who started it with an unforgettable try from a scrum twenty yards out. With the entire Springbok back row (including van Wyk) and his opposite number converging on him he veered outwards and flashed past all of them, plus an apparently stock-still full-back, to score a magnificent try between the posts.'

Greenwood and O'Reilly's tries took the Lions to 23–11, but back came the Springboks with tries by Swart and Koch. In the third minute of injury time Briers sidestepped his way over for what seemed to be a match-winning try but van der Schyff missed a straightforward conversion. The Lions had won by a single point. There were many sparkling moments in the game with Morgan, Butterfield and O'Reilly's tries deserving special mention. Lions manager Jack Siggins voiced the felings of all present when he said, 'Never have I played such a hard game of rugby – even if I was sitting in the grandstand.'

'One of the greatest Welsh outside halves ever', Cliff Morgan kicks for touch against France in Cardiff in 1956. His fellow Welsh players are (from the left) Geoff Whitson, Onllwyn Brace and Bryn Meredith

(Press Association)

16 VIVE LA REVOLUTION

Wales 6   France 16   (Cardiff Arms Park, March 28, 1958)

It doesn't take an archaeologist to date France's emergence as a great rugby nation.

Though they had been part of European rugby's elite since the early years of the 20th century, they were serial underachievers. Reporters at *L'Equipe* and *Midi Olympique* used to have a field day, pointing the finger after some embarrassing and spineless defeats. Yes, the game had caught the public's imagination in France in the 1920s but it was the domestic club competition which aroused French passion, not the fortunes of the national team.

All that changed after their historic first win at Cardiff Arms Park in 1958 – after 50 years of trying. A sequence of match-winning performances followed which made the rest of the world stand up and take note. Here was a new-look French side shorn of its disciplinary issues, weaknesses of temperament and missed opportunities. Thanks to their inspirational captain, Michel Celaya, and master technician, Lucien Mias (the doctor from the Mazamet club who was affectionately known as 'the bulldozer with a brain') they had a plan and played every match with resolve and purpose.

The 1957–58 season had started disastrously for the Tricolores with defeats against Scotland and England (their sixth consecutive Championship defeat). In desperation the selectors turned to the Lourdes club and included their entire three-quarter line for their match against the Wallabies in early March. They also decided that the inspirational second-row forward Lucien Mias should be given carte blanche as far as team tactics were concerned. The Wallabies, who had narrowly lost to all four home countries, were comprehensively thrashed 19–0 by France in front of a disappointing crowd of only 15,000 at Stade Colombes.

France arrived in Cardiff full of confidence and with high expectations. However, Clem Thomas's XV hadn't lost a match all season, and when the team was announced – Carwyn James playing alongside Malcolm Thomas in the centre, and Cliff Morgan making his final appearance in a Welsh jersey – there was a huge demand for tickets.

On a bright, sunny day Wales started promisingly but at half-time the teams were all square at 3–3. In the second half, however, the French forwards were ruthless, allowing Antoine Labazuy from Lourdes to control proceedings at outside half. The press reports following France's 16–6 victory were most complimentary, especially of their attractive style of football. One of J.B.G.

'The bulldozer with a brain', France's Lucien Mias grabs a loose ball at Cardiff in 1958.

(Press Association)

Thomas's statements in the *Western Mail* was particularly pertinent: 'Even Cliff Morgan could not hold the Welsh side together against such an organised and determined effort.'

The victories against Australia and Wales opened up a new chapter in French and world rugby. Mias and his band of brothers continued on their triumphant march when, to everyone's amazement, they took the series against the Springboks, drawing the first Test and winning the second 9–5 at Ellis Park, Johannesburg. They became the first team since 1896 to win a Test series in South Africa.

France's progress was further confirmed in the 1958–59 season when they became the first French team to win the Five Nations title outright. As John Griffiths had it in *The Phoenix Book of International Rugby Records*, '... a refreshing new dimension was added to the international scene by the ebullient French. Fast interpassing forwards who peeled from lineouts in a formidable wedge-shaped pattern launched many attacks from which dynamic backs and mobile forwards were able to penetrate opponents' defences'.

The Tricolores were a match for anyone. What is more, they had brought to the game a new brand of the game: champagne rugby.

Taking the game to Wales at the Stade de France in 2015, French forwards Thierry Dusautoir and Uini Atonio, inheritors of the robust ball-handling tradition started by Lucien Mias. (Press Association)

Ieuan Evans, one of Wales's greatest ever wing three-quarters, tries to evade New Zealand's Va'aiga Tuigamala for the Lions in the second Test of the 1993 series. Trying to keep up is second-row forward Martin Johnson. Like their 1959 counterparts, the '93 Lions only managed one victory in a closely-fought Test series.

(Press Association)

17 'WE WUZ ROBBED'

New Zealand 18   British Lions 17   **(Carisbrook Park, Dunedin, July 18, 1959)**

No one likes to lose and no one likes a loser. As a child, I was often told off because I couldn't stand losing at Monopoly or Cluedo – 'It's only a game' they said. Whatever… But there are times when I had to concede my opponent was better than I was. Mind you, losing also made me reflect on those 'if only' moments: the referee's decision, the bounce of the ball and the hundred other little things which didn't go my way.

The worst defeat for any sportsman or woman is, however, when you feel you have been really hard done by. That's when congratulating your opponents can only be done through gritted teeth, and when you want to shout 'We wuz robbed'!

So it was in 1959 when, for the first time on an overseas tour to New Zealand and Australia, the *Western Mail* and *The Sunday Times* decided they would send their rugby correspondents to follow the team and keep the British public up to date on progress via regular reports from J.B.G. Thomas and Vivian Jenkins respectively.

When the team for the first Test was announced everyone knew what the tactics would be – attack, attack, attack. The back line was a veritable list of stars which included Tony O'Reilly, Peter Jackson, Malcolm Price and Ken Scotland. But they needed the ball. This is where the forwards played their part, with the likes of R.H. Williams, Syd Millar, Noel Murphy and Gordon Wood in the van.

It was R.H. Williams who told me all I needed to know about that travesty in Dunedin. And he knew a thing or two. After the Lions series in South Africa in 1955, the home side's management had said that RH was good enough to play for the Springboks, whilst the New Zealand management of 1959 followed suit by declaring that he would have made the All Blacks team that year.

That first Test was played on a sunny afternoon at Carisbrook Park before a crowd of 41,500 with thousands more packed onto the railway embankment nearby, as A.L. Fleury blew his whistle for the start of one of the most controversial matches of the era. After half an hour the All Blacks led 6–3, two Don Clarke penalties to one from the boot of David Hewitt for the Lions. Five minutes before half-time a Bev Risman break created space for Hewitt who had Tony O'Reilly on his shoulder. The winger's pace took him to the try line before Clarke could lay a finger on him. With half-time approching fly-half Risman launched a kick for wing three-quarter Peter Jackson to chase. As the ball

Dr Syd Millar, British Lion prop in 1959, who would later coach the 1974 Lions and become Chairman of the IRB.

Don Clarke, the New Zealand full-back who beat the Lions single-booted in Dunedin in 1959.

J.J. Williams scores at Eden Park during the second Test at Eden Park, Auckland in 1977. Nearest to him is All Black scrum-half, Sid Going , whilst his supporting Lions in red are Brynmor Williams (9), Ian McGeechan (13) and Andy Irvine (15). As in 1959, however, the Lions lost the series 3–1.

(Colorsport)

stood up inches short of the try line Jackson and several New Zealand defenders overran it but the supporting Malcolm Price touched down effortlessly. The visitors were 9–6 ahead at the interval. The crowd which had been on its feet in appreciation of the Lions' attacking style was a little more subdued now that their team was behind!

The Lions' third try came ten minutes into the second half when Peter Jackson raced over for his second try, but from this point onward the match was dominated by Mr Fleury's whistle. The visitors were penalised at every opportunity allowing Clarke to keep the home side in contention with a succession of penalties. With ten minutes left to play, the Lions scored another try. When McMullen, the New Zealand centre, dropped a pass, Bev Risman was there to boot the ball on. Full-back Ken Scotland was onto it in a flash, and in one movement delivered a pass to Malcolm Price who crossed for a fourth try for the Lions. Risman's conversion resulted in a lead of eight points for the visitors.

But the penalties kept on coming until it was only 17–15 to the Lions. In Vivian Jenkins's book *Lions Down Under* the validity of Clarke's fifth penalty goal was questioned: 'Mick English, the Lions touch-judge kept his flag down for this one, but the referee had other ideas. Some of us, I must confess, wondered if the ball had gone outside the post'.

And there was one more to come. Thus it finished: Don Clarke's boot 18, Lions 17!

More heartbreak in Carisbrook, this time in 1983 as All Black fly-half Wayne Smith steps inside Ollie Campbell with Gary Whetton in support. The Lions in pursuit are (from left to right) Jim Calder, Mike Kiernan and try scorer John Rutherford. Shades of 1959, the Lions scored more tries than New Zealand in this third Test, but still lost 15–8.

(Colorsport/Colin Elsey)

18 D.K. Saves the Day

South Africa 3   British Lions 3   (Ellis Park, Johannesburg, June 5, 1962)

D. Ken Jones, 'a beautifully balanced runner'.

(Press Association)

As a schoolboy in the early 1960s, I would spend most of the summer holidays either fishing in the local streams or playing tennis on the public courts at Gwaun-cae-gurwen. But even then, rugby football was never far away.

This was especially true of the summer of 1962, when the British Lions were on tour in South Africa and we would rush to the local newsagent to find out how our heroes were performing. I also have a vague recollection of watching brief highlights of the 1962 Lions on our black-and-white television. Images still appear in the sub-conscious: of fly-half Richard Sharp suffering a broken cheek bone after a dangerous crash tackle by Mannetjies Roux in the match against Northern Transvaal; of second-row forward Keith Rowlands plunging over for what would have been an equalising score in the second Test at King's Park, Durban. The referee, however, insisted he was unsighted and blew for full time.

But it was centre D. K. Jones who captured the imagination during the first Test at Ellis Park. Late in the first half the Springboks had taken the lead when Jones had failed to find touch, giving wing three-quarter Roux the opportunity to counter-attack, change direction and feed centre John Gainsford who ran the wide arc to the corner for a crucial unconverted try. However, with only minutes of the match remaining, Ken made amends with a try which remains to this day as one of the finest in the annals of Lions history.

Normally Lions full-back John Wilcox would have gathered the bouncing ball and kicked to the safety of his near touchline. However, realising that something quite desperate was required to save the match, he decided to run across field. Yes, he was tackled, but somehow, he managed to transfer the ball to fly-half Gordon Waddell who made some progress before slipping a short pass to Ken Jones. Taking possession at pace he outstripped the close defenders before moving into overdrive. A beautifully balanced runner, the Llanelli flyer sidestepped left-wing Taylor, lengthened his stride and prepared to take on full-back Lionel Wilson. With uncanny judgement he jinked infield and then sprinted the final 25 yards to the line.

The crowd were on their feet. They had witnessed a phenomenal try.

John Gainsford, star centre and scorer of the Springbok try at Ellis Park.

(Press Association)

19 ALL BLACK AND AMBER

Newport 3 New Zealand 0   **(Rodney Parade, October 30, 1963)**

In the days before the regional sides, the powerhouses of Welsh rugby were the clubs. Among their finest hours were triumphs over international tour teams. Swansea in 1935 and Cardiff in 1953 both beat New Zealand. Llanelli famously did the same thing in 1972. As did Newport. Indeed they were the only team of any description to defeat the 1963–64 All Blacks.

The game was played during what was half-term week for schools in Glamorgan, a week which I spent receiving athletics coaching at Ogmore under the guidance of Ron Pickering, the man who would steer Lynn Davies to Olympic gold in Tokyo in 1964. The BBC had decided to broadcast the second half of the match live from Rodney Parade and all at Ogmore tuned in to support the Black and Ambers. The All Blacks had won their opening two games quite comfortably but were well aware that Newport, under Brian Price's captaincy, would be difficult opponents. When the visitors team was announced, it was almost a full-strength Test side and included the likes of Don Clarke, Ralph Caulton, Ian MacRae, Earl Kirton, Kevin Briscoe and Colin Meads, not to mention a world-class back row in Tremain, Nathan and Lochore.

Newport were forced into a late change at wing forward when Brian Cresswell withdrew with a leg injury, to be replaced by 19-year-old Keith Poole from Blaenavon who had only made his debut three days earlier against the Wasps. Poole, who never played for Wales, has the unique honour of appearing against three major touring teams without losing once: New Zealand 1963 (3–0), Australia 1967 (3–3) and South Africa 1969 (11–6).

On a wet and windy October afternoon in front of 25,000 spectators the Newport forwards, right from the kick-off, dominated proceedings. Brian Price was a towering presence in the lineout and was an inspirational figure around the field. The Black and Ambers showed no respect for their illustrious opponents at the scrummage where their front row of Johnson, Bevan and Jones won eight heels against the head. British Lion flanker Glyn Davidge was simply immense, continually putting his body on the line.

With the All Blacks on the back foot, the mercurial David Watkins was given carte blanche to control play and his meticulously weighted diagonal kicks and up-and-unders caused problems for New Zealand's back three. With the weather deteriorating by the minute, it became obvious that the game would be a low-scoring affair, to be ultimately decided by a defensive error or a moment of magic.

David Watkins, Wales and British Lions outside half, a key component of the Newport team who beat the All Blacks in 1963.

(Press Association)

The hero for the home side was centre three-quarter John 'Dick' Uzzell, who had managed to get time off from his studies at St Luke's College to visit his sick father in hospital. Halfway through the first half Stuart Watkins's cross-kick created an attacking platform for Newport. From the resulting maul, scrum-half Bob Prosser fed Uzzell who initially considered racing for the corner but then checked and dropped a goal which wasn't the prettiest but cleared the bar right in front of referee Gwyn Walters.

It was cut and thrust from both sides for the remainder of the match but Newport held the initiative and were by far the better side. 'A 3-0 score didn't do us justice,' said Uzzell in a post-match interview. The first to congratulate him was his father whose recovery can only be described as quite remarkable!

When I joined Cardiff in the mid 1960s, I was privileged to play numerous matches alongside Dick Uzzell after his transfer to the Arms Park side. During a distinguished career he won five caps for Wales but will forever be remembered as the man who dropped the winning goal against the All Blacks!

The airborne All Blacks perform the haka at Rodney Parade before losing to Newport in 1963. (Press Association)

20 WHINERAY ON HIS WAY

Barbarians 3 New Zealand 36   (Cardiff Arms Park, February 15, 1964)

'Which is the greatest All Blacks team of all time?' Opinions are expressed, votes are cast but, more often than not, no definitive answer is given. Instead what we are left with is a list of questions:

'How much do we really know about Dave Gallaher's 1905 squad?'

'How good were the opposition when Cliff Porter's team went undefeated on their long tour to the Northern Hemisphere in 1924?'

'Who would bet against David Kirk's World Cup winners of 1987?'

'Wasn't the Richie McCaw XV which demolished the British and Irish Lions in 2005 better than all these?'

It's like asking 'Who's the better tennis player, Federer or Borg?' Different eras throw up different geniuses.

Since hanging up my boots in 1978 I've visited New Zealand on numerous occasions and have been constantly asked – 'Gareth, you've played against the All Blacks! Which team impressed you the most?' But I've never been able to settle the argument. Even in defeat against the Lions in 1971, Colin Meads's team, for example, was a formidable unit.

But, ultimately, early impressions count, which is why I always find myself paying tribute to the New Zealand team I saw in action as a young schoolboy back in 1963–64 – a team captained by prop forward Wilson Whineray, a truly inspirational leader and described as 'second to none of the great captains who have come from overseas'. Most of the games I saw were on television but I travelled to the Arms Park along with 45,000 other supporters to see the Cardiff match. The tourists were hell bent on revenge having lost to the Blue and Blacks ten years earlier by 8–3 when Sid Judd and Gwyn Rowlands crossed for match-winning tries. In 1963, Cardiff's dependable goal-kicker Alun Priday had left his kicking boots at home and Whineray's men scraped home by a single point thanks to a Don Clarke penalty and a Mac Herewini drop goal.

Having won 32 of the 34 matches played (they lost to Newport 3–0 and drew 0–0 against Scotland) the popular tourists travelled to Cardiff for their final match against the Barbarians.

Supporters from far and wide were desperate for tickets – who could forget the Baa-Baas magnificent victory over Avril Malan's Springboks just two years previously. Could such a victory be repeated? It seemed so when veteran Kiwi prop forward Ian Clarke, playing for the Barbarians, caught brother Don's kick

It used to be one of rugby union's iconic fixtures, but sadly Barbarians v New Zealand matches have become all but obsolete. The last time they played was in 2009, when Ben Smith (top) and Bryan Habana went head to head.

(Press Association)

out of defence, called for the mark and kicked a quite superb drop goal from 40 yards.

The Barbarians competed bravely during the first half but were overwhelmed in the second period when the All Blacks cut loose in a try-scoring feast of rugby much appreciated by a capacity crowd of 60,000. The final try was real Roy of the Rovers stuff. With referee Gwyn Walters looking at his watch, the ball was moved along the line towards Wilson Whineray, whose handling skills could have seen him playing in the back row or in the back division (he once played as a half-back). He raced towards full-back Stuart Wilson and with Ralph Caulton outside him delivered the text-book dummy and raced in under the posts. The crowd went wild and erupted into a rendition of 'For He's a Jolly Good Fellow'.

In true Arms Park tradition the crowd invaded the pitch and carried Whineray shoulder high off the field. He later described it as 'the greatest day of my rugby career'.

Wilson Whineray is fourth from the left in this picture, which shows Babarians prop Ian Clarke (himself an All Black) tackling his fellow countryman Colin Meads at Cardiff in 1964. Clarke dropped a famous goal that day. (Press Association)

21 SHARP'S SHOW AND HANCOCK'S HOUR

Twickenham Tries, 1963 and 1965

Those schoolboy memories keep flooding back, and more often than not, they're memories of Wales scoring tries – against England!

I can still picture (from a distance) Dewi Bebb scoring at Cardiff in 1959, on his debut as a player and my debut as a spectator. The pitch resembled a quagmire as Bebb threw into the lineout, took a tapped return from lock R.H. Williams and with a swerve and a shift left England's Peter Jackson and Jim Hetherington behind him on his way to the game's solitary score. Little did I think then that eight years later I would be playing alongside Dewi in his final game for Wales, when he would again touch down during a 34–21 demolition of the old enemy.

But, to be fair, there are English tries which live in the memory, too. Richard Sharp's score in the 1963 Calcutta Cup match against Scotland at Twickenham was, in Cliff Morgan's words, twenty-two seconds of rugby magic.

'All grace, pace and co-ordination', Richard Sharp touches the ball down to score England's winning try against Scotland in 1963.

(Press Association)

His pace over the first few yards created the opportunity, before he executed the perfect dummy scissors with Mike Weston to confuse the Scottish defence. With wing three-quarter Jim Roberts in support outside Sharp, Scotland's last line of defence, Colin Blakie, was caught in two minds. Sharp took advantage, leaning away from Roberts with a glorious dummy before crossing the try line. I watched the action on television but Cliff Morgan who was at Twickenham was always in raptures about Sharp's effort. Whenever we discussed great tries, he said, 'Gareth bach, it was all grace, pace and co-ordination – for a fly-half watching a fly-half, this try was the ultimate!'

It was another try scored at Twickenham two years later, however, which stands out. Again it was in a Calcutta Cup match, but at the end of an indifferent season for both teams, the Wooden Spoon was also up for grabs. With Her Majesty the Queen in the Royal Box and with only a few minutes remaining, Scotland were leading 3–0 thanks to a David Chisholm drop goal as the vistors scented their first win at Twickenham since 1938. When Scottish wing David Whyte was tackled in the opposition's 25, England's Mike Weston gathered and immediately released Andy Hancock on the left wing with the opposition try line a million miles away. What happened next has become part of rugby folklore, or as J.B.G. Thomas put it, 'Hancock simply galloped into history!'

The Northampton wing three-quarter was initially hesitant but soon realised he was in space and increased his speed. He beat Iain Laughland within inches of the touchline and away he went over the halfway line. According to JBG in his book *Fifty Two Famous Tries*, Hancock then stumbled, changed course and swerved infield all within a few strides. The crowd rose in anticipation as he desperately looked for support, acutely aware that the Scottish defence was approaching from all directions.

As Stuart Wilson closed in for the tackle, Hancock sidestepped away from him and set off for the try line 30 yards away. His weary legs could hardly carry him but with blue jerseys in pursuit he dived over the line.

The conversion was missed but it hardly mattered as the teams shared the spoils. At the time, no one had run further for a try in an international match.

Andy Hancock, scorer of one Twickenham's most spectacular solo efforts.

(Press Association)

22 SOUTH SEA SPARKLE IN SOUTH WALES

Wales 28 Fiji 22   **(Cardiff Arms Park, September 26, 1964)**

Fiji never featured in the geography curriculum at Pontardawe Grammar Technical School (or at Millfield for that matter!) so I knew very little about those visitors who toured Wales, France and Canada in the autumn of 1964.

Their visit was the brainchild of the Welsh Rugby Union secretary, W.H. (Bill) Clement, who was aware of Fiji's flair-filled approach to the game, but whilst the WRU agreed to finance the tour, there was general disappointment when the International Board refused to sanction their game against Wales as a full international.

The five matches the South Sea islanders played in Wales attracted record attendances, as the visitors proved they were worthy opponents. 55,000 came to watch their 'international' at the Arms Park against a Welsh XV, and were enthralled as Fiji kept the ball in hand for the best part of 80 minutes.

The newspaper headlines on the Monday morning paid tribute to their happy-go-lucky attitude: 'Fijians win 55,000 friends in defeat' and 'This was a step into the past, to the days of the Golden Era when rugby was a handling game'. Meanwhile Frank Tinsley, the sports editor of the *Fiji Times and Herald* more than captured the mood: 'The Welsh XV tasted Fijian unorthodoxy and were often caught flat-footed and dumbfounded'.

Fiji ran, counter-attacked and threw caution to the wind and the crowd just loved it. Wales to their credit entered into the spirit of the occasion and contributed to a rugby spectacle which thrilled the crowd. To this day I still remember Alun Pask throwing a one-handed dummy before diving over for a try. There were many thrilling moments and as the game was broadcast live it became one of the most talked about sporting events of the year.

The game produced 13 tries. And though Fiji played most of the match without their lock foward Nalio who had been forced from the field with a dislocated shoulder, they were undeterred, even managing to score three tries and 13 points in the last ten minutes. Remarkably the prop forward Sevaro Walisoliso grabbed a hat-trick.

Five years later I captained Wales against Fiji at Suva in another magnificent spectacle. This was a new experience for all of us – we had never before been cheered by fans hanging from the palm trees surrounding the ground! That day the talented Welsh three-quarters played Fiji at their own

Alun Pask, who out-Fijied the Fijians at Cardiff in 1963 with his one-handed dummy and dive.

(Press Association)

game and in the end we proved too strong for the home side. It was a different story in 1970, however, when I played for the Barbarians against the islanders at Gosforth in the company of J.P.R. Williams, Fergus Slattery, Phil Bennett, David Duckham, Barry Llewelyn and John Spencer. We were firm favourites but Fiji had no respect for reputation. We were taught a rugby lesson and were eventually overwhelmed by their relentless attacking policy. All we could do at the final whistle was congratulate them on a phenomenal performance: they had scored seven tries to our two!

You just cannot take Fiji for granted – just ask Wales's 2007 Rugby World Cup side!

Wales 34 Fiji 38! Akapusi Qera seems to be laughing out loud as he leads the charge at Nantes during the Rugby World Cup in 2007, 44 years after the trademark Fijian combination of dexterity and physicality won so many friends at Cardiff.

(Press Association)

23 THE WHIP IN THE WRISTS OF KEN CATCHPOLE

The Scrum-half Master Class of 1966

According to Benjamin Franklin, 'an investment in knowledge pays the best interest'. As I look back at my career, I can now recognise moments when I learnt so much about the game from those around me, when the knowhow of others impacted directly on my skillset.

1966–67 proved to be a significant season for me as a young rugby player. I'd just started a three-year teacher-training course at Cardiff College of Education and in September made my debut for Cardiff RFC against Coventry. They were exciting times and within two months I was included in the Probables XV, partnering David Watkins, in a trial match at Maesteg. The game was staged in order to help the national selectors choose a Welsh team to play against Australia in December. Unfortunately, I wasn't selected to play against the tourists for Cardiff or for Wales, which at the time was a huge disappointment. However, it proved to be a blessing in disguise as it gave me the opportunity of watching Ken Catchpole at close quarters, one of the great scrum halves of the modern era.

I wasn't the first nor the last sportsman to have studied the style of the stars. In recent times, hundreds of young goal-kickers will have modelled their technique on Jonny Wilkinson's, whilst boys and girls from Barcelona to Buenos Aires will have spent hours and hours trying to mimick the moves of Lionel Messi.

During Australia's 1966 tour, I was privileged to watch Ken Catchpole and his fly-half partner Phil Hawthorne in action. I remember very little about the games against Cardiff and Wales as I kept an eagle eye on the play of the Australian half-backs.

Ken Catchpole was an extraordinary scrum-half, his very strong forearms and wrists enabling him to whip the ball away with little or no backward movement. Phil Hawthorne is on record as saying how his partner's passes reached him with lightning speed from set pieces giving him extra moments in which to weigh up his options. Catchpole once admitted that positioning was the element of the game upon which he had concentrated most as he developed his speed of pass. I can honestly say that watching Ken Catchpole in 1966 was a rugby education for me personally and with his development of the spin pass he gave scrum-halves like Chris Laidlaw and myself another dimension to our game.

John Thornett, captain of the 1966–67 Wallabies, is chaired off by Ken Catchpole's half-back partner Phil Hawthorne (right) and Barbarians captain Noel Murphy at Twickenham. (Press Association)

For the Welsh match at Cardiff, Catchpole took over as captain from the injured Thornett for a game which Australia had no realistic hope of winning. Or so the press said. They had never previously beaten Wales but the gifted scrum-half inspired his team-mates to a 14–11 victory. They went on to beat England at Twickenham next, after which Catchpole was described as 'the greatest scrum-half the world has known'. No Welshmen would have gone quite so far: Haydn Tanner was also a bit special!

What makes a memorable moment in rugby? Usually it's a try or a break or a desperate tackle, but sometimes all it takes is a pass. And watching Catchpole and his pass was one of the great rugby moments of my early career.

'A rugby education': Australian legend Ken Catchpole about to whip the ball away against England in 1967.

(Press Association)

24 JARRETT'S MATCH

Wales 34   England 21   **(Cardiff Arms Park, April 15, 1967)**

It was Keith Jarrett's match from kick-off to final whistle. The 18-year-old rookie, who had only just completed his studies at Monmouth School, became an 18-year-old superstar in the space of 80 glorious minutes. I can vouch for this as I was there, actually there on the pitch, to witness it all.

Many beforehand had questioned the selectors' wisdom in naming a young unknown for such a high-profile game – and in a position which was alien to him – so those selectors must have heaved a collective sigh of relief at the final whistle as their decision was vindicated.

The 34–21 result must also have come as a huge relief to the young Jarrett, bearing in mind that he had had a nightmare experience a week earlier when he had been asked by the national selectors to play out of position at full-back for Newport against Newbridge at the Welfare Ground. His performance that day was so poor that it led to David Watkins, the Newport captain, moving him to his customary centre three-quarter position at half-time. One can only imagine what this did to his confidence in the days leading up to the match against England at the Arms Park.

As it turned out everything went right for young Jarrett. He confessed in a post-match interview, 'If that first penalty kick, which hit the post and glanced over had bounced back out, it all might have been different.' However, it was the try which brought the house down, only the second time in Welsh rugby history for an international full-back to cross the try line.

During the first half our captain David Watkins had waved the inexperienced full-back to stand deeper in defence. With Wales leading 19–15, the England centre three-quarter Colin McFadyean kicked towards the North Stand touchline from midfield near his 25-yard line at the Westgate Street end. Jarrett, having heeded his skipper's advice, gathered the bouncing ball at full pace, and sprinted fully 50 yards to score a simply sensational try underneath the main scoreboard. England's defenders were lost in his wake, staring in wonder. He went on to score 19 points in the match, equalling Jack Bancroft's total against France at St Helen's in 1910.

I was there and I was privileged to have been there!

Keith Jarrett, who became an 18-year-old superstar in the space of 80 minutes. (Colorsport)

25 THE KING AND I

Wales 30   England 9   (Cardiff Arms Park, April 12, 1969)

Barry John, 'effortlessly off the cuff'.   (Colorsport)

In 1972, Barry John's retirement from the game at 27 years of age would shock the rugby world. When he confided in me some weeks prior to the official press release, I spent hours and hours trying to get him to change his mind, but in vain. He had already decided to accept attractive offers from the media and business communities.

Whenever people ask me about Barry, I have a stock answer: 'It's not how good he was; it's how good he could have been!' His feats for the British Lions in New Zealand in 1971 had made him one of the game's superstars, but I honestly feel that an even more glittering future lay ahead of him.

For six years I had been given an exclusive view of Barry's genius, as his half-back partner for Cardiff, Wales, the Lions and the Barbarians. We went well together, the King and I, even if we had contrasting styles, they say: Edwards, dynamic and macho; John, effortlessly off the cuff. If one of us was having an off-day then the other would usually make a point of pulling out a little bit extra.

What Barry John had more than any other player I ever saw was time on the ball, time to take in the options around him with a wide-angle glance, and time to do his thing, the devastating break or precision punt. He sized up and he struck, often going for the opposition's jugular, as when he tormented Fergie McCormick in the first Lions Test at Dunedin with long, raking touchfinders which continually rolled just beyond the full-back's grasp.

However, a more creative Barry John moment was the one at Cardiff Arms Park in 1969 when Wales hammered England. It was the day when Maurice Richards equalled the Welsh try-scoring record of four in a game. Although the scores were level at half-time, we eventually went on to register our biggest win against the old enemy since 1922.

Barry's try at the start of the second half was pure magic and what I, as captain, witnessed on that glorious sunny day has stayed with me as one of the truly great Barry John moments. John Taylor picked up a loose ball in midfield and transferred to the supporting Keith Jarrett who was himself closely marked by the England centres John Spencer and David Duckham. Keith's deft left-footed chip took him clear of the opposition but his hurried pass was slightly behind John Dawes and Maurice Richards. It seemed as if the movement was doomed but the maestro from Cefneithin appeared from nowhere, scooped up the ball and spotted a gap.

He ghosted, he glided, he weaved, coming off his left foot and his right foot, to leave the likes of Bob Hiller, Trevor Wintle, Rod Webb and Budge Rogers in an embarrassed heap as he crossed the try line. It was a moment of individual brilliance. It was Barry John.

Cardiff Arms Park, 1969: time for Barry to honour his pledge to catch it when I throw it! The head-dressed Irishmen are Ken Kennedy (left) and Mike Molloy, while the two Welshmen far left are Brian Thomas and Mervyn Davies (with headband). (Colorsport)

England full-back Bob Hiller, seen here kicking for goal against Ireland in 1972, was part of the embarrassed heap of defenders left in Barry John's wake at Cardiff in 1969.

(Press Association)

*Paying homage to the King. All Blacks Sid Going (left)
and Ian Kirkpatrick have eyes for Barry John (10) only
as I get my pass away at Lancaster Park in Christchurch
during the second Test of the 1971 Lions series.*

(Colorsport/Peter Bush)

There was only one Gerald Davies:
a genius, no less. (Colorsport)

26 GERALD OF WALES

Scotland 18   Wales 19   **(Murrayfield, February 6, 1971)**

Ah, the 1970s: Abba, Watergate and Welsh rugby! Both J.P.R. Williams and I played in every single match of every single Grand Slam in 1971, 1976 and 1978, and they were all memorable occasions for us. But time seems to have told us that of them all, 1971 was maybe the most special, because it was our first such success for 19 years.

The 1970–71 season started in fine style with a comprehensive 22–6 victory over England at Cardiff Arms Park – it was the first time since 1912 for Wales to take the lead in the series of matches against the old enemy. Historically, the game in Edinburgh was always fraught with danger and we were more than aware of what happened in 1951 when a Welsh team labelled 'Invincible' crashed to a 19–0 defeat against Peter Kininmonth's warriors.

Murrayfield 1971 was one of the great occasions of my rugby career – a true rugby classic! Scotland could have won, it fact at one stage should have won. If Peter Brown's routine conversion of Chris Rea's try in the dying stages had been successful then Scotland would have been two scores ahead with only five minutes left to play. As it was, they were only four points ahead.

Above the cacophony of a fever-pitch Murrayfield, we just about heard skipper John Dawes's words of reassurance as we made our way towards the halfway line for the restart, 'There's still time. There's still time'. I had no idea that the chemistry graduate was a master of psychology but his timely words spurred us into action.

Scotland soon had a lineout on their own 25-yard line. All they had to do was secure possession and clear their lines. Peter Brown called for a long throw. Frank Laidlaw didn't hear him and lobbed the ball to the front of the line, where Delme Thomas managed to palm it into my waiting hands for one last-ditch attack. The ball shot along the line to J.P.R. Williams who released Gerald Davies. As he approached full-back Ian Smith, Gerald glided effortlessly outwards in a parabola and crossed for a splendid try. 18–17 to Scotland with a conversion to decide the outcome of the match.

The responsibility for taking the kick was given to John Taylor, a naturally left-footed kicker. An eerie silence descended as 80,000 nervous spectators held their breath. I was standing near the halfway line next to Delme Thomas who was in a sorry state; he was facing his own posts unable to keep still! The brown-leather Gilbert ball sailed through the uprights and the noise returned redoubled! At the restart I made an attempt to seal the victory with

Delme Thomas leaps highest at Murrayfield in 1972, challenged by Gordon Brown (with headband) and Rodger Arneil. The two no. 2s are Jeff Young (left) and Frank Laidlaw. (Press Association)

a speculative drop goal from long range which just sailed wide. We were carried from the field of play on a sea of red. Looking back, it was a shame that one side had to lose as it had been such an exciting encounter.

Wales went on to win the Grand Slam, thanks to a 23–9 victory against Ireland in Cardiff and a hard fought 9–5 win against France at Stade Colombes, Wales's first victory in Paris for 14 years.

But it is Gerald's try that stays with me. In my estimation he was a genius. Originally an attacking centre three-quarter for Cardiff, he was encouraged by coach Clive Rowlands to switch from midfield to the wing on the Welsh tour of Australasia in 1969 and quickly realised that he was tailor-made for the position.

He was the complete footballer who revelled in the counter-attacking philosophy employed at the time. His pace (quite devastating over the first 15 metres) and mercurial sidestepping mesmerised the opposition. His three tries in the 1971 British and Irish Lions Test series in New Zealand, his four tries against Hawke's Bay on the same tour and another four at Pontypool Park in a Schweppes Cup match were testament to his outstanding ability. In layman's terms, 'There was only one Gerald Davies!'

En route to the Grand Slam, the Wales team who beat Ireland in Cardiff in 1971.
Back row (left to right): Barry Llewelyn, Mervyn Davies, Mike Roberts, Denzil Williams, Delme Thomas, Dai Morris, coach Clive Rowlands.
Middle row (l. to r.): J.P.R. Williams, John Bevan, Barry John, John Dawes, John Taylor, Gareth Edwards, Gerald Davies.
Front row (l. to r.): Jeff Young, Arthur Lewis
(Press Association)

27 'KIRKIE': MIGHTY NOT MEAN

New Zealand 22   British Lions 12 (Lancaster Park, Christchurch, July 10, 1971)

I'm often asked, 'Who's the best scrum-half you've ever played against?' I could provide a short list which includes the likes of Sid Going at international level and Alan Walters of Bridgend at club level. But I prefer to convince the questioner that my main concern prior to kick-off was always the composition of the opposing back row. Scrum-halves I could handle. Three athletic hard cases dedicated to the task of my discomfort were another matter!

After all it wasn't I who nullified Going in the third Test of the 1971 Lions tour to New Zealand. No, that was the work of blind-side wing forward Derek Quinnell. 'Shadow Sid for eighty minutes' was Carwyn James's pre-match instruction. And that's what Derek did. It's what back rowers do!

Skrela, Bastiat and Rives; Tremain, Lochore and Williams; Greyling, Bedford and Ellis; Lamont, Goodall and Slattery; Lister, Lochore and Kirkpatrick – five quite outstanding back-row units I had to face during my international career and believe me they were truly world class. However, the best individual I ever played against, indeed one of the game's great players, was Ian Kirkpatrick.

Ian's try against the Lions in the second Test at Lancaster Park, Christchurch in 1971 was among the best scored during the last century or any century for that matter. A fierce maul was in progress near the halfway line. Suddenly, the awesome figure of 'Kirkie' emerged clutching the ball in one hand and brushing me away with the other. Seconds later he was wrong-footing JPR and that, believe me, was no mean feat. He went on to outpace David Duckham, Barry John and Mike Gibson in his quest to reach the corner flag. My dismay was tempered by the conviction that, whatever else the flanker did in his career, in those dramatic moments he had established an undying claim to greatness.

It was a privilege to play in the same team as Ian Kirkpatrick for a World XV against South Africa in 1977 and I can therefore testify to the enormous support he gave the scrum-half behind him. It is also worth mentioning one other quality of Ian Kirkpatrick's that is by no means shared by every sportsman: I never saw him do a mean or underhand thing on the field.

Ian Kirkpatrick, the best back-row foward I played against.

(Colorsport)

Another world-class wing forward, Jean-Pierre Rives in the wars against Wales in 1983.

(Colorsport)

J.P.R. Williams, seen here kicking ahead against New Zealand at Cardiff in 1972, dropped a series-winning goal for the Lions at Auckland in 1971, much to everyone's surprise!

(Colorsport)

28 JPR the Drop Goal Star

New Zealand 14   British Lions 14   (Eden Park, Auckland, August 14, 1971)

KGB, SAS, CIA. Three organisations capable of causing international mayhem and destruction. In Wales, however, we have our own three-letter acronym of terror: JPR!

J.P.R. Williams is in my humble estimation one of rugby's all-time greats. I know I'm biased but I also suspect that I'm well qualified to volunteer that opinion as I had the honour of playing with and against him. Since his retirement other great full-backs have graced the international scene – players of the calibre of Andy Irvine, Serge Blanco, Christian Cullen, Gavin Hastings and Matt Burke, not to mention the current crop of stars like Israel Folau, Israel Dagg, Leigh Halfpenny, Rob Kearney, Mike Brown and Stuart Hogg.

However, if I were asked to select a World XV, I would have no hesitation in selecting JPR as my full-back. Some of the 15s listed above are or were sensational attacking runners but whilst admiring their skills I still have to say that JPR's defensive qualities allied to his attacking guile, superb positional play and deceptive speed made him the most formidable presence, a real titan.

JPR distinguished himself for club and country and continued playing for local side Tondu as a flank forward into his fifties. Although excelling at tennis and squash it has to be said that he gained most satisfaction from playing rugby union. He very rarely kicked, but ironically it was his one and only drop kick at international level which proved crucial for the British Lions against the All Blacks in 1971. After our convincing third Test win at Wellington, a win or a draw at Auckland in the final match would see us win a series in New Zealand for the very first time. It soon became apparent that Colin Meads's men weren't going to go down without a fight and raced into an 8–0 lead.

However, the Lions's character soon came to the fore in a fiercely contested match. At the start of the second half we were ahead 11–8 thanks to a Peter Dixon try – he was at my shoulder to take a scoring pass when the All Blacks panicked near their own line. Barry John's conversion and two penalty goals provided the impetus required but New Zealand were not to be outdone and levelled the score with a Tom Lister try. Laurie Mains surprisingly missed the conversion.

Halfway through the second half, following a forward drive, David Duckham threw a one-handed pass infield to JPR in acres of space. In an instant the full-back took aim and fired a towering drop goal from all of 50 yards. 14–11 to the Lions! Before kick-off, John had casually mentioned to

A rare sight: JPR looks worse for wear as Lions captain John Dawes supports him at Wellington during the third Test of the historic 1971 series.

(Colorsport/Peter Bush)

fellow full-back Bob Hiller, 'Watch out for a drop goal!' When the kick sailed over, JPR turned to the main grandstand to give a thumbs-up sign in the direction of an incredulous team-mate, who just happened to be one of the finest kickers of his era!

We managed to dominate the final twenty minutes of play but also wasted several golden scoring opportunities. A Laurie Mains penalty equalled the score but when the final whistle went it mattered not – the Lions had won the series 2–1.

Leigh Halfpenny, another Welsh full-back to have distinguished himself for the Lions Down Under, is brought to ground by Australia's Digby Ioane at Brisbane in 2013.

(Press Association)

29 Worldbeaters

England Slay the Southern Hemisphere Giants

The 1960s and 1970s were decades of disappointment for the England rugby team. The selectors chopped and changed, and in 1967–68 used 28 players in five matches, with Bob Lloyd and Peter Larter the only two players who were retained for the entire season. The 1970–71 centenary season should have been one of celebration, but proved disastrous as England were outclassed in four of the six matches played.

Season 1971–72 was no better when for the first time ever they lost all four of their championship matches, contributing to their longest period of failure since the breakaway of the northern clubs in 1892. The game's founders had become the game's laughing stock.

And yet, in an 18-month period between June 1972 and November 1973 England achieved what had seemed impossible. They defeated South Africa 18–9 at Ellis Park, Johannesburg, New Zealand 16–10 at Eden Park, Auckland (the All Blacks' first defeat at the ground since 1959) and Australia 20–3 at

The might in white: Chris Ralston (with kneeband) and Stack Stevens, two of England's ever-presents during their slaying of the three Southern Hemisphere giants. Here they contest possession with Australia's Mike Cocks (6) and Rex L'Estrange at Twickenham in 1973, watched by team-mates Fran Cotton (far left) and Andy Ripley (with headband).

(Press Association)

Twickenham! It was an astonishing record. Wales had never beaten South Africa, whilst England had just humbled the Sprinboks for a second time in three years, having also won 11–8 against Dawie de Villiers's team at Twickenham in 1969.

In South Africa in 1972 England ended an unbeaten tour with a famous Test victory, thanks to four penalties and a conversion from the boot of new cap Sam Doble and a try from Bristol flyer Alan Morley. Shock waves reverberated throughout the rugby community when Peter Squires, Stack Stevens and Tony Neary crossed for tries to stun the All Blacks at Eden Park in 1973. John Pullin then became the first international captain in rugby history to win tests against South Africa, New Zealand and Australia when, three months later, they defeated Australia at Twickenham. Seven players featured in all three matches – Pullin, Alan Old, Stack Stevens, Chris Ralston, John Watkins, Andy Ripley and Tony Neary.

To this day neither Wales, Ireland nor Scotland have matched England's magnificent feat of winning a Test match in South Africa and New Zealand. Enough said.

Chris Ralston, again in the thick of it, winning lineout ball against New Zealand's Samuel Strahan at Eden Park, Auckland in 1973.
(Colorsport/Peter Bush)

30 HOW, WHY, WHEN AND WHERE?

Barbarians 23   New Zealand 11   **(Cardiff Arms Park, January 27, 1973)**

Over forty years after the event, it's still talked about the world over.

How many of you have heard of the Generator and Bear pools on the Varzuga river in Russia? They are among the most productive salmon pools in the world, so when a few of us gathered at the nearby village in a wooden hut (or 'saloon', as they called it), I wasn't expecting rugby union to be the centre of attention. Apparently, the village had been built in 1665 and to be honest nothing much had changed since the reign of Tsar Alexis I! We were sipping our vodkas when the mayor, a former atomic submarine commander, approached the TV set and announced, 'Gareth, we are going to look at *the* match!' Well, everybody else watched a VHS video of the 1973 Baa-baas/All Blacks match, whilst I, subdued by vodka, slept on an adjacent bench!

'David. Tom David…' The Llanelli and Wales wing forward plays his celebrated part in the famous 1973 Barbarians try against New Zealand, as fellow back rower Fergus Slattery tries to get in on the act. (Colorsport)

'John Dawes. Great dummy...'
The Barbarians captain looking inside, as
Derek Quinnell (with headband) prepares
to enter proceedings in support of Tommy
David (not pictured). Redundant on the
right is All Blacks prop Kent Lambert.

(Colorsport)

In Britain and Ireland, of course, we seem to be celebrating 'that match' continuously. I know I'm always being asked 'How?', 'Why?', When?' and 'Where?''. It even prompted a question recently by Ian Kirkpatrick, the All Black captain on the day and a great friend of mine: 'Why do you still celebrate the victory? Afer all it was just an ordinary match; it wasn't a Test match!' I tried to explain that it was a backhanded compliment to the All Blacks because of their standing in the rugby world. I should have told him, 'Ian, taking your scalp at any time is a real achievement'.

While visiting Hamilton in 2003, I met Alistair Scown, the former All Black flank forward. It was he who had failed to tackle Phil Bennett in the Barbarians 22 at the beginning of the move which led to the dramatic try that saw me dive over the line in the left-hand corner. 'Oh! no', he said, 'do we have to talk about that match?' 'Alistair', I replied, 'You've made a lot of people happy as a result of that try!'

When I look at that try today I'm intrigued by the number of instances when things could have gone horribly wrong. A pass could have been delayed; the ball could have gone to ground. It was a series of improvisations which kept the movement alive and eventually resulted in one of the finest displays of attacking rugby in the game's history.

The Barbarians had selected a strong team, all but two having been part of the victorious 1971 Lions tour to New Zealand. It was an opportunity for the British public to see their heroes in action. The All Blacks, on the other hand, wanted to prove that they were still a force to be reckoned with. They had a point to prove on away soil.

Our preparations on the training ground at Penarth were disastrous as we dropped the ball, over-ran each other and threw a series of ill-judged passes. Gerald Davies pulled a hamstring and was replaced by John Bevan, whilst Mervyn Davies developed influenza on the morning of the match which brought Tom David in as flanker with Derek Quinnell moving to No. 8. And yet on the day magical offloads by David and Quinnell proved crucial.

During the making of a DVD to celebrate the match, Phil Bennett, David Duckham and I re-lived the buzz of the occasion and could now appreciate the fantastic tries scored by both teams. However, we all agreed that the period which won the game for us was the twenty minutes after half-time when our defence kept the All Blacks at bay. Happy memories!

Celebrating on the shoulders of jubilant fans after the Barbarians have defeated New Zealand for the first time ever. And it's a match we've been celebrating ever since! Also caught up by the crowd is All Blacks captain Ian Kirkpatrick (far left).

(Colorsport)

'That match' wasn't all about grace and glamour; the two packs got stuck into one another also. Here Graham Whiting looks to offload from a lineout, even if Willie John McBride and, next to him, Sandy Carmichael (far right) have other ideas. The rest of the forwards forming an orderly queue are (left to right) Tom David (obscured), Alex Wyllie, Bob Wilkinson, Peter Whiting, Kent Lambert, Ray McLoughlin and Hamish MacDonald. The hunched figure is All Blacks hooker Ron Urlich.

(Colorsport)

Prodigious points scorer and counter-attacker Andy Irvine, Scottish full-back and Lions Test wing in South Africa in 1974. Andy was a dangerous opponent and a great team-mate.

(Colorsport)

31 THE CELT ON THE VELDT

South Africa 9   British Lions 28   (Loftus Versfeld, Pretoria, June 22, 1974)

When the British Lions embarked on the tour of New Zealand in 1971, even the most optimistic supporter had to agree that we were the underdogs. To return, therefore, as victors to a reception at Heathrow which would have done the Beatles proud was something that I will never forget.

The downside to all of this, however, was that the expectation to beat the Springboks in 1974 was now at an all-time high. Fans would stop me in the street and with the usual greetings would also be the challenge, 'You won in New Zealand – now go and beat the Boks!' While I was grateful for the confidence that the rugby public had in the team, I also had to remind them that playing South Africa on their home turf presented many different challenges – the rarefied atmosphere at altitude, the rock-hard grounds and the never-say-die attitude of the home team, to name but a few.

'Over to you, Gareth…' The 1974 Lions boasted a pack as formidable as any to have left our shores and included this particular human shield: (from the left) Bobby Windsor, Fran Cotton, Ian McLauchlan, Roger Uttley, Gordon Brown and Mervyn Davies.

(Colorsport)

While we were sitting in the departure lounge at Heathrow, I looked around at the personnel selected for the tour. There was a nucleus of very experienced players, buoyed by the success of the previous tour now straining at the leash, raring to get on the plane and take on the Springboks. I too felt quietly optimistic. There was healthy competition amongst the squad – Andy Ripley and Mervyn Davies would fight it out for the No. 8 shirt, for example, whilst Alan Old and Phil Bennett were rivals at outside half.

It was on this tour that Phil came of age: a world-class player who had stepped out of Barry John's shadow. In the second Test at Loftus Versfeld in Pretoria, he was at his brilliant best. You could say that the hard grounds in South Africa were tailor-made for him. Not only was he lightning quick off the mark, he had a sidestep which completely flummoxed his opponents. The try Phil scored in that game was a peach. Near the halfway line Fergus Slattery, with a perfect pass, set

Skipper Willie John McBride gives me a congratulatory headlock after the third Test victory which clinched the 1974 series in South Africa.
(Colorsport)

'99', the Lions' famous call to arms in 1974 at the 'Battle of Boet Erasmus'. J.P.R. Williams (with headband) has run in from full-back with typical enthusiasm. For one reason or another, I don't seem to be in the picture…
(Colorsport)

Phil on a course for the Springbok 22. With some clever sidesteps he left several men in green in his wake before completely baffling full-back Ian McCullum with an outrageous dummy. The try was the culmination of a fabulous individual movement and we, as players, could only compliment him on his genius. Marvellous!

J.J. Williams was another Welshman who excelled on those hard grounds. He scored two tries in that 28–9 victory at Pretoria. The first was a team effort which began with a counter-attack by Phil from his own 22, a curving, sidestepping run followed by quick passing along the line from McBride to Mervyn, back to McBride, Gordon Brown to yours truly. As the move gathered momentum, I had no choice other than to kick towards the right-hand touchline where Roger Uttley thanks to some surprisingly deft footwork managed to keep the ball in play. Here there was a moment's hesitation as some thought that the ball had crossed the touchline, but suddenly JJ appeared from his customary left wing position, booted the ball on and eventually swooped for the score.

In this instance Phil had been the instigator but on several other occasions he was the one who executed the moves – a true craftsman, a master of his art.

Relishing the hard ground, J.J. Williams sprints over for the first of his two tries in the third Test at Boet Erasmus, Port Elizabeth, much to the delight of local fans.

Phil Bennett, 'master of his art'.

Driving the Springboks back at Port Elizabeth on the day we became the first Lions team since 1896 to win a series in South Africa.

(Colorsport)

'In the mould of Barry John': Hugo Porta strokes the ball elegantly to touch against an England XV in 1978.

(Colorsport)

32　KICKS AND PORTA

Wales 20　Argentina 19　　　　　　　　**(Cardiff Arms Park, October 16, 1976)**

Sometimes you just know you're in the presence of sporting greatness. When Martina Navratilova stepped on to court, when Tiger Woods strode down the fairway, when Pele had the ball at his feet, there was a sense of anticipation. These are the kind of sportsmen and sportswomen who can generate excitement even before the curtain is raised. One such rugby player was Hugo Porta.

During the 1970s none of the other Five Nations teams managed to beat Wales at Cardiff. However, there was one afternoon when I genuinely believed we were about to be humbled on our own sacred turf by one of the world's emerging nations. Argentina were ahead of Wales with the clock ticking down in injury time. However, a high tackle on J.P.R. Williams allowed Phil Bennett to kick a penalty goal which gave us a 20–19 victory. We were mightily relieved, but it was an Argentinian player who won all the plaudits. Hugo Porta gave Terry Cobner, Trevor Evans and Mervyn Davies the runaround that afternoon, and I was not surprised when Merv named Porta as the best outside half he had ever played against.

In 1977 I had the pleasure of playing with him in a series of celebration matches involving a World XV in South Africa. He was an elegant player in the mould of Barry John and liked my delivery to be exactly where Barry had wanted it: just far enough in front to make him stretch. His footwork was clever and his strong hips allowed him to withstand the efforts of hard-tackling flankers. He is also remembered for his match-winning place kicking, not least during South America's victory over the Springboks in 1982 at Bloemfontein. The Jaguars' 21 points all came from Porta, who put over four penalties, a dropped goal and a conversion, besides crossing for a try.

The *Sunday Telegraph* rugby correspondent John Reason described Porta as the 'sleepy eyed Clint Eastwood waiting to erupt from under his sombrero', whilst Carwyn James, after seeing Porta in action for Argentina against Wales 'B', stated in his Friday column in *The Guardian*, 'For a critic or a coach or ex-fly half, it was a question of having one's faith restored in the aesthetic and artistic possibilities of backplay'.

As physically imposing as he was athletic and quick, John Kirwan on his way to the try line against France during the inaugural Rugby World Cup final at Auckland in 1987.

(Colorsport Colin Elsey)

33 SERGE AND SWERVE

Blanco and Kirwan Make their Mark on the World Stage

The Rugby World Cup is now universally regarded as one of the premier events in world sport.

Back in 1987 New Zealand were the undisputed winners of the inaugural competition beating France 29–9 in Auckland. Several other countries also contributed to a feast of rugby, amongst them Wales, Fiji, Australia and Scotland, who held finalists France to a 20–20 draw in the pool stages at Christchurch. Wales claimed third place thanks to a last-minute try by Adrian Hadley and a match-winning touchline conversion from the boot of the dependable Paul Thorburn.

I have two abiding memories of that month-long rugby extravaganza. Firstly, France and Australia locked at 24–24 with only minutes remaining of a classic semi-final confrontation as the *Tricolores* launched a last-ditch effort in an attempt to reach the final. This they did in typical Gallic fashion with Charvet, Rodriguez, Berbizier and Lagisquet keeping the ball alive against all the odds. At one stage, it seemed as if a Lynagh interception had stemmed the flow and for an instant we all thought the movement was over. However, Rodriguez picked up the loose ball and fed Serge Blanco who was supporting within a few feet of the touchline. Monsieur Blanco, one of the most potent attackers of his era, considered his options and with five Australians converging set off for the try line. It was the stuff of legends. Would he… wouldn't he? The line was in sight. Could they… couldn't they? He dived. He stretched. He got there! Unbelievable drama.

The other memory is of the All Black wing John Kirwan blazing a trail which took him to a tally of six tries in the tournament. He was one of the new breed of wingers – as physically imposing as he was athletic and quick. His try against Italy in one of the group matches was simply breathtaking. He collected a kick-off deep in his own 22 and set off on an 80-metre dash leaving the Azzurri defenders in turmoil. It really was an awesome sight – Kirwan with the ball tucked under his left armpit beating man after man with deft swerves and searing pace. I'm pretty sure he ran through the entire Italian team! If Blanco's was the best collective effort, then Kirwan's was the individual try of Rugby World Cup 1987 and brought him instant stardom.

Although Wales came a creditable third in the competition, they were steamrollered by New Zealand in the semi-final losing 48–3 in a one-sided contest. John Kirwan in the space of eleven months played in three matches

New Zealand's David Kirk becomes the first captain to lift the William Webb Ellis trophy

(Press Association)

against Wales notching up a personal tally of eight tries. He is recognised in his native land as one of the finest right wing three-quarters to wear the All Black jersey.

Last-minute drama, as befits a Rugby World Cup semi-final: France's Serge Blanco beats Tommy Lawton's desperate dive to seal Australia's fate at the Concord Oval, Sydney in 1987.

(Colorsport/Colin Elsey)

34 STADE DE TWICKERS

England 21 France 19 **(Twickenham, March 16, 1991)**

Conflicts between England and France have always been ferocious. They are the stuff of legendary battlefields: Hastings, Agincourt and Waterloo. How ironic then that a French assault on English soil in 1991 should have done more for the Entente Cordiale than any prime minister or president.

At a Twickenham centenary dinner in 2009 the guests present voted Philippe Saint-André's 1991 try as the best ever scored at the historic venue and he was duly presented with a piece of silverware, having beaten in the process folklore favourites like Prince Obolensky, Richard Sharp, and Andy Hancock. It was a score described in the *Daily Mail* as 'fashioned by adventure and executed by genius'.

England full-back Simon Hodgkinson insists to this very day that he had a hand in the movement which raised Twickers to its rafters. His penalty attempt in the sixth minute drifted past the far post and was casually collected by scrum-half Pierre Berbizier. I remember watching the match on television and everyone, including the cameraman and the England players, relaxed momentarily expecting the inevitable grounding of the ball prior to a restart.

Simon Hodgkinson's missed kick for goal led to the best try ever scored at Twickenham. On his hands and knees is Franck Mesnel, as his co-centre Philippe Sella watches Hodgkinson kick ahead. Behind the two Frenchmen is Jeremy Guscott.

(Colorsport/Andrew Cowie)

Serge Blanco (right) and Jeremy Guscott challenge for a high ball at Twickenham in 1991. It was Blanco who took a chance that day, and created history.

(Colorsport/Andrew Cowie)

But, hey, this was France and before you could say 'Napoleon Bonaparte' the ball was in Serge Blanco's hands. His philosophy was a simple one – take a chance and create history. Although still positioned deep in his in-goal area, Blanco immediately released another of France's great unpredictables, Jean-Baptiste Lafond, who lengthened his stride and passed on to the incomparable Philippe Sella (one of my all-time favourite centres). Sella drifted infield throwing a delightful pass across his body to fly-half Didier Camberabero who was supporting near the touchline. The England defenders were now alive to the threat posed by the *Tricolores*. Camberabero, running at pace, miraculously chipped the ball over Rory Underwood's head, caught it in his stride and had the presence of mind to cross-kick in the hope that a player in a light-blue shirt might be positioned to take advantage. One such was Philippe Saint-André who allowed the ball to bounce twice before gathering and haring over for the inevitable try beating Jeremy Guscott's despairing last gasp attempt to derail him. Commentator Nigel Starmer-Smith described it as a sensational try and I can only agree.

Although France scored two more tries through Camberabero and Franck Mesnel, it was England who were triumphant at the final whistle with Will Carling's men winning their first Grand Slam in eleven years. Wild celebrations followed but, remarkably, 25 years after the event, it's Saint-André's try which is still the talk of the town.

Still the talk of the town: French players celebrate Philippe Saint-André's epic score.

(Colorsport/Andrew Cowie)

An 'extraordinary talent', David Campese on his way to the line during the 1991 Rugby World Cup at Cardiff. The forlorn Welshmen are Arthur Emyr (left) and Mike Hall.

(Press Association)

35 THE MAZY CAMPESE

Australia 16   New Zealand 6   **(Lansdowne Road, Dublin, October 27, 1991)**

Wizard, virtuoso, maestro – all words used by rugby writers all over the world to describe the genius that was David Campese.

Born of Irish Italian parents, his mother's family (part of the Murphy clan) sailed from Kinsale to New South Wales at the turn of the 20th century, whilst his father left Montecchio, a village between Venice and Padua at the age of 21 with the sole intention of seeking a new world and way of life. Just think, young David could have distinguished himself in the green of Ireland or even dazzled for the Azzurri!

In his book *Sporting Century*, Frank Keating sings the praises of Campo: 'His acceleration allowed him to burst through the tiniest chink', whilst Gerald Davies in *The History of the World Cup* recognises coach Bob Dwyer's role in accommodating Campese's needs: 'He was allowed the freedom to run at will. But the essence of his extraordinary talent was recognised within the team and allowances made for it'.

Personally, I feel that David Campese is one of the finest rugby players to have graced this noble game of ours and his tally of 64 international tries tells its own story. He was a Scarlet Pimpernel who was given the licence to appear here, there and everywhere. Of course he had electrifying pace and superb

Not even New Zealand's John Kirwan can stop Campese going in at the corner during the Rugby World Cup semi-final at Lansdowne Road.

(Press Association)

timing, but he also had that X Factor which made the impossible appear probable. He never, ever died with ball in hand, his delightful passes to supporting team-mates opening up the tightest defences. David Campese was a joy to behold.

Two of his most telling performances were at Lansdowne Road in 1991, the first when he inspired Australia to a dramatic last-minute win against Ireland in the Rugby World Cup quarter-final and then when he went on to destroy New Zealand in the semi-final, a match I watched open-mouthed from the stands. Australia scored two tries against the Kiwis, the first after seven minutes an individual try of brilliance when Campese latched on to Nick Farr-Jones's pass in centre field near the New Zealand 22-metre line. The All Blacks stood off momentarily waiting for a pass, or a Campo goose-step or change of pace, but all he did was accelerate, maintaining a diagonal course towards the All Black corner flag. Two New Zealand defenders at last reacted decisively but it was too late as the man from Manley kept his composure and streaked over the line.

Australia's second try saw Campese collect Michael Lynagh's ambitious kick ahead and set off on yet another of his mazy runs. On this occasion, some 15 metres from the try line, he was surrounded by All Blacks but somehow managed a blind, over-the-shoulder pass which released Tim Horan for the try. Game, set and match to the Wallabies.

Within minutes of losing to Ireland in the 1991 quarter-final, Michael Lynagh's try saves the day for Australia. David Campese (obscured) sits it out! The other players are (from left to right) Tim Horan, Peter Slattery, tackler Jack Clarke, Brendan Mullin, Gordon Hamilton, Ralph Keyes, Jeff Miller, referee Jim Fleming and Brian Robinson.

(Press Association)

36 TRY FROM THE END OF THE WORLD

New Zealand 20   France 23   (Eden Park, Auckland, July 3, 1994)

There are certain moments which never seem to fade with time.

For the followers of French rugby, July 3, 1994 will go down in the annals as a date to rival the storming of the Bastille on July 14, 1789. It was when the all-conquering All Blacks were themselves conquered by a brilliant French side who became the only team, other than the Springboks and Lions, to win a series in New Zealand. Philippe Saint-André's men had won the first Test of two at Lancaster Park, Christchurch 22–8 (Jonah Lomu's debut and Philippe Sella's one hundredth appearance) and as a result of that reversal the All Blacks were under intense pressure from the media and supporters alike to produce a winning performance at Eden Park. The ground in Auckland has always been a fortress for New Zealand rugby and Sean Fitzpatrick's men were quietly

Philippe Sella, captain of France when New Zealand were beaten in their own backyard in 1994, passes out to Émile Ntamack.

(Press Association)

Jean-Luc Sadourny, scorer of 'the try from the end of the world'. (Press Association)

confident, well aware that they'd only lost nine matches at the venue since 1921.

The home side were virtually at full strength with players of the calibre of John Kirwan, Jonah Lomu, Frank Bunce, Stephen Bachop, Ian Jones and Zinzan Brooke included in coach Laurie Mains's line-up. France on the other hand had suffered injuries and were forced to play Philippe Saint-André at centre and fly-half Thierry Lacroix on the wing. With just three minutes remaining New Zealand were leading 20–16 and seemed set for a win. However, one moment of *Tricolore* magic remained.

When All Black fly-half Stephen Bachop kicked deep towards the opposition goal line, he had reckoned without Philippe Saint-André. Gathering the loose ball in a flash, the Frenchman accelerated past Matthew Cooper and Sean Fitzpatrick, before being upended near the French 10-metre line by lock Mark Cooksley. France's abrasive hooker Jean-Michel Gonzalez was on hand to pick up and find Christophe Deylaud in support. The fly-half made ground before finding Abdelatif Benazzi on his shoulder. The movement was by now gathering pace and Benazzi's delayed pass to wing Émile Ntamack was perfectly timed. He handed on to open-side wing forward Laurent Cabannes who, with three defenders converging, veered towards the far touchline before releasing the supporting Deylaud with a switch pass which had 'Try!' written all over it. The fly-half's swerving run created panic in a stretched All Blacks defence and as he passed to scrum-half Guy Accoceberry the end was nigh! The pharmacy graduate could have scored himself but he gave the ball to full-back Jean-Luc Sadourny who crossed for the winning try.

At the post-match press conference the French captain Saint-André labelled it 'a counter-attack from the end of the world' and in time it became known as 'the try from the end of the world'. In 2003 *Daily Telegraph* readers voted the try the fourth best of all time in either code of rugby.

The 1994 defeat was a seminal moment in All Blacks history as they haven't lost a match at Eden Park since!

A fair cop! French players in their changing room at Eden Park celebrate their historic series win, led by P.C. Philippe Sella.

(Colorsport)

This was history: Nelson Mandela presents the William Webb Ellis trophy to Springboks captain Francois Pienaar after the 1995 Rugby World Cup final. (Press Association)

37 42 MILLION SUPPORTERS

South Africa 15   New Zealand 12   (Ellis Park, Johannesburg, June 24, 1995)

As someone who has taken part in international sport, I've had the privilege of witnessing several iconic episodes. But none has moved me like the moment I saw Nelson Mandela wearing the No. 6 Springbok jersey, dancing and hugging Francois Pienaar as they celebrated the home team's victory in the Rugby World Cup. This was history.

Ellis Park, Johannesburg had never seen anything like this outpouring of emotion and it was the culmination of five years of revolutionary change in the country. It was on February 11, 1990 that a 71-year-old Mandela walked free from his 27-year incarceration. His crime had been to oppose injustice in his homeland, but thanks to his humanity and powers of forgiveness, sweeping changes were implemented in South Africa which eventually led to the tearing down of racial segregation.

'I lift up my eyes': Joel Stransky has just struck the world-cup winning drop goal. Looking the same way, but hoping against hope, are (left to right) All Blacks Andrew Mehrtens, Josh Kronfeld and Walter Little. (Press Association)

August 15, 1992 saw the official acceptance of the Springboks back into the international rugby fold. Two years later Mandela was elected President and in 1995 the Rugby World Cup was staged in South Africa – no mean feat considering everything that had gone before. In addition to being a huge international sporting event this would also be seen as a symbolic occasion to unite all the different inhabitants of the country.

Unquestionably, one of the stars of Rugby World Cup 1995 was New Zealand's left wing of Tongan descent, Jonah Lomu. His statistics for the tournament spoke for themselves. Seven tries in five matches including four in the semi-final against England. That match at Newlands, Cape Town became known as the Jonah Lomu match.

England's semi-final nemesis Jonah Lomu is tackled by Springbok scrum-half Joost Van der Westhuizen during the final at Ellis Park, Johannesburg. (Press Association)

A nation celebrates: South African flags unfurled at Ellis Park. (Press Association)

His huge physical presence and blistering speed made him an impossible opponent and Will Carling's men had no answer to this juggernaut. As we left the stadium at the end of the match, I remember someone asking me, 'Have you seen anyone like him?' My answer was, 'Yes but he had a No. 4 on his back!'

New Zealand were firm favourites to win the final at Ellis Park but the magnitude of the occasion was not wasted on Francois Pienaar and his men. It wasn't a classic encounter but it was the result everyone wanted. New Zealand looked to Jonah Lomu but he was closely marked throughout, and in extra time Joel Stransky, who had controlled play admirably, struck the decisive dropped goal to win the Webb Ellis Cup.

This was more than rugby; this was a giant step taken towards the unification of a country. 'Fantastic support from 65,000 South Africans at Ellis Park,' remarked David van der Standt to Francois Pienaar at the post-match interview. The Springbok captain immediately corrected the interviewer saying, 'David, we didn't have the support of 65,000 South Africans. We had the support of 42 million South Africans.' To me, it was one of the greatest days in the history of rugby union.

38 OF AMATEURS, SHAMATEURS AND PROS

Vernon Pugh and the Blazer Brigade

Vernon Pugh, rugby union's greatest ever administrator.

(Press Association)

Intrigue was in the air when the letter arrived by special delivery. It was an official invitation from the Australian Rugby Union to attend a high-profile match at the Sydney Football Stadium on July 31, 1993, as part of rugby's efforts to welcome South Africa back into the international fold. Other former players had received similar invitations, amongst them Sir Colin Meads, Jacques Fouroux (who would later introduce us to bottles of Château d'Yquem) and Jim Renwick.

The itinerary made for interesting reading. We were to travel on business-class flights, an experience I'd never had as a player, and booked to stay in a five-star hotel overlooking the Sydney Harbour Bridge. There would be 500 guests at the dinner, including representatives of some of Australia's major companies. We were all curious: why had we been summoned?

That question was answered by the evening's compere: 'We look forward to resuming our rivalry on the field whilst off the field the visit of the Springboks will also help swell the coffers of the Australian rugby team. It was a brazen statement. Was the amateur game being dismantled, the game as I'd known it? Rugby union was certainly on a rollercoaster ride but would the International Rugby Board be able to hang on to it?

Fast forward two years. Three rugby union presidents, Louis Luyt of South Africa, Richie Guy of New Zealand and Leo Williams of Australia, meet for coffee at the Sandton Sun Hotel in Johannesburg. It is the day before the Rugby World Cup Final at Ellis Park. They subsequently announce at a press conference that Rupert Murdoch's News Corporation is prepared to hand over $555 million for the rights to televise Southern-Hemisphere rugby for the next ten years. There is no mention of how much the players will receive. Ross Turnbull, the Australian Rugby Football Union's representative on the IRB, has already started recruiting players from both Northern and Southern Hemisphere countries. Without the support of the players Turnbull realises that Murdoch's deal would be doomed to failure.

Two months later in Paris, the IRB officially announces that it is abandoning its amateur ethos, and the game is declared open.

Who, however, made all this possible? Vernon Pugh QC, a man with a razor-sharp intellect, hailed from the anthracite-mining village of Glanaman in the Amman Valley and he knew his rugby. In a bearpit of powerful individuals, representing influential and often self-interested bodies, all jostling aggressively for positions, it was he who outsmarted and outmanoeuvred them all. As a leading figure with the IRB, Pugh had been only too aware that those national bodies at the time were ill-equipped to run the game. The game cried out for leadership; the IRB had to embrace professionalism. For once the blazer brigade listened.

I remember asking him whether he and his colleagues had any choice at the famous Paris meeting in 1995? Could they have turned their backs on professionalism and insisted the game remain amateur? His answer was immediate: 'If the IRB had put its head in the sand and said it is staying an amateur game, we would have had a professional game controlled by interests outside the sport such as entrepreneurs and broadcasters. They would have looked at the possibility of a TV product and put some new laws into the game. What we would have ended up with would have been a hijacked, hybrid version of rugby union and rugby league. It would have been delivered for a global audience and would have been a very different sort of game'.

Vernon Pugh was a man with a vision and in a short space of time proved himself to be rugby union's greatest ever administrator. (It was he also who brought Italy into the Six Nations, set up the Heineken Cup and brought in a structure which established seven-a-side as a global game.)

The changes allowed rugby union players to be paid for their services. Previously the players had been pawns in a game where everyone seemed to be benefiting except those emerging from the dressing rooms on a Saturday afternoon. Unions and committees, in both hemispheres, were obsessed with making money, whilst the players were being asked to turn out regularly for their clubs and countries, and all for a meal and a few pints of beer at the final whistle! It really was a mad, mad world.

It was Vernon Pugh who restored its sanity.

Throwing caution to the wind, Scotland's Gregor Townsend scorches through to score in Paris in 1999. (Press Association)

39　THE TOONIE FLIP

Gregor Townsend's Paris, 1995 and 1999

'Cometh the hour, cometh the man!' they say – except in Paris, of course!

With only three minutes remaining of a pulsating contest at Parc des Princes on February 18, 1995, Scottish skipper Gavin Hastings, following a break in play, called his team together for some words of encouragement: 'All we need to do is score a try under the posts.' And then he turned towards the man mostly likely to do just that: 'OK, Gregor?'

Gregor Townsend, who had made a major contribution to the Scottish effort with an earlier try, was at this point feeling somewhat below par. Minutes earlier his misdirected kick had flown into the waiting hands of Philippe Saint-André whose resulting try had put France 21–16 ahead. But here was a chance for him to redeem himself and secure victory for Scotland.

Outside half Craig Chalmers released the ball along the back line and a deft step inside from Townsend completely wrongfooted the French defence. The man from Galashiels was eventually held, but before going to ground managed to give what can only be described as a quite remarkable one-handed reverse pass to Gavin Hastings who found himself in acres of space. The full-back ran the 40 yards to the posts and his try gave Scotland a dramatic 23–21 victory, their first in Paris for 29 years. It was the stuff of legends.

I witnessed the winning try on *Rugby Special* on the Sunday evening, and couldn't fail to be impressed by that pass (the Toonie Flip, as it became known) and the win. As a former player, I know from experience that playing France at Stade Colombes or Parc des Princes was as tough as they come. In fact whenever I have the pleasure of fishing or playing golf north of the border, that great Scottish achievement is always a topic of discussion.

Fast forward to 1999 and Scotland were at it again, on this occasion at the newly opened Stade de France in St Denis. Gregor Townsend, after his starring role in the British and Irish Lions success in South Africa in 1997, was now restored to his favoured position at fly-half. He was often portayed as a maverick, but to me this was a huge compliment: rugby needs players who can produce the unorthodox and create opportunities when all seems to be lost.

Scotland's 1999 win by 36–22 stunned the rugby world. They played breathtaking rugby scoring five tries in a purple patch at the end of the first half with Alan Tait and Martin Leslie claiming two apiece. Gary Armstrong's men attacked relentlessly with Townsend on several occasions throwing caution to the wind and counter-attacking from his own 22. His try, Scotland's third, was a gem as he took on the defence with pace and purpose. With the Parisian sun beating down, Scotland produced their greatest half of rugby ever with coach Jim Telfer at the final whistle putting it all into perspective: 'It seemed as if the other team weren't on the park!'

About to execute the Toonie flip, Gregor Townsend senses that Gavin Hastings (far right) is alive to the opportunity in Paris in 1995. The French defenders are Christophe Deylaud and Thierry Lacroix (12). The Scottish onlooker is Ian Jardine.

(Colorsport)

40 THEY THOUGHT IT WAS ALL OVER

Wales 32   England 31   (**Wembley Stadium, London, April 11, 1999**)

When Wales claimed a late victory at Murrayfield in 1971, everyone talked about John Taylor's magnificent touchline conversion which led to a 19–18 win. Gerald Davies's try which preceded the kick was conveniently forgotten. Ironically, when Scott Gibbs crossed for a try in the second minute of injury time against England at Wembley in 1999, it was the well-built centre who was the talk of the town. However, it was Neil Jenkins's conversion which secured a 32–31 victory for Wales. Such are the ways of rugby union football!

I was part of the S4C commentary team for that extraordinary match at Wembley Stadium, a match England should have won by a country mile. During our half-time deliberations, we asked 'How are we still in this game?' Coach Graham Henry also conceded in his post-match interview that 'England

No way through at Wembley – this time. Scott Gibbs is held up by Lawrence Dallaglio and Neil Back (7), as Mike Catt and Scott Quinnell (8) move in. Meanwhile, behind them, Matt Dawson seems to be dancing!

(Press Association)

Cling on! Jonny Wilkinson tries to haul back the irresistible Scott Quinnell, hoping that Barrie-Jon Mather will come to his rescue.

(Colorsport)

were the better side. We didn't play well but we hung on in there.' Lawrence Dallaglio's men, going for a 12th Grand Slam and a fifth successive Triple Crown, should have made sure of victory. Had they been, possibly, too sure of themselves? In sport, as in life, cockiness can become arrogance which can often lead to disaster.

Most England supporters were still confident of victory with only minutes remaining. They were leading 31–25 and in our purpose-built studio high above the iconic playing surface, the producer asked me to be brief whilst summarising – 'We're joining Channel 4 for the racing within minutes of the final whistle.' It suited me down to the ground as there was very little to say about the Welsh performance. I jotted a few words on my notepad: 'Dallaglio's men still dominating possession… England toying with us, possibly displaying over confidence… England decide not to go for goal from a penalty… Can't believe it!'

Yes, Wales hung on in there, and as spectators from both sides were in the process of leaving early, the match was turned on its head when the men in red launched a final attack. Sounding like a firm of solicitors, Wyatt, Howley and Quinnell combined to create space for the marauding Scott Gibbs. A juggled ball, two sidesteps and a swerve plus a single-handed salute whilst diving over the whitewash saw the Pencoed product score an iconic try. Minutes later Neil Jenkins coolly slotted the conversion for a single-point victory!

It might well be a disservice to Scott Gibbs to suggest that he will purely be remembered for that Wembley try, as he achieved so much more as a player in both codes. However, for all those Welshmen present on that glorious April day in 1999, it will almost certainly be his legacy.

'That glorious April day…' Scott Gibbs about to touch down for that unforgettable try at Wembley, as Martin Johnson (4), referee Andre Watson, Jason Leonard, Victor Ubogu, Colin Charvis and Jonny Wilkinson maintain a respectful distance.

(Colorsport)

Anno Dominici! It's definitely France's year as Christophe Dominici rounds New Zealand's Christian Cullen during his team's dramatic comeback in the Rugby World Cup semi-final in 1999.

(Press Association)

41 MAY THE FORCE BE WITH YOU

France 43   New Zealand 31   **(Twickenham, October 31, 1999)**

Before the semi-final stages of the 1999 Rugby World Cup, New Zealand under Taine Randell's captaincy, were quietly confident of getting to the final and winning the Webb Ellis Cup for the second time in their history.

So it was that all roads led to Twickenham for the second semi-final between New Zealand and France. (Australia had already reached the final the previous day after their narrow 27–21 extra-time victory against South Africa the previous day). The 1998–99 Five Nations season had been a disastrous one for the French with Raphael Ibanez's XV ending the campaign with the wooden spoon. They had progressed to the semi-finals with victories against Canada, Namibia, Fiji and Argentina – hardly adequate preparation for a full-on contest with the mighty All Blacks! I, along with 70,000 other spectators, felt that France had no realistic hope of winning – New Zealand were the odds-on favourites.

Some five minutes into the second half, the All Blacks were in the ascendancy – they led by 24–10 with man-mountain Jonah Lomu crossing for two tries after typical barnstorming runs. His second was his 15th in Rugby World Cups. But in a sudden and unexpected turnaround the *Tricolores* added 26 points in a frantic 15-minute period. One of their stars was outside half Christophe Lamaison who had been originally overlooked by the selectors but was included at the last minute following the withdrawal of the injured Thomas Castaignede.

Lamaison's kicking was just phenomenal – he did not miss a single kick all afternoon, and ended the match with a personal tally of 28 points which included a try, 4 conversions, 3 penalties and 2 dropped goals. His clever chip over the New Zealand defence also created a try for Richard Dourthe. The three French tries in the second half were the result of typical Gallic flair, passion and optimism, with backs and forwards working in total harmony. The best was saved till last when Andrew Mehrtens lost possession in France's 22. The ball was hacked on initially by Lamaison, chased and then kicked on further by the fleet-footed flanker Olivier Magne. At the very last minute he was overtaken by left wing Philippe Bernat-Salles who got to the try line before full-back Jeff Wilson.

Days prior to the big match, French wing Christophe Dominici (who collected a fortuitous bounce and streaked over for France's second try) was quoted as saying, 'We have to be honest and admit that out of ten matches against New Zealand we would probably lose eight or nine times, but in a World Cup semi-final you never know; you might be swept along by a superior force'.

France's found that force and their comeback stunned the All Blacks and the rugby world. It was a classic confrontation and described by all who saw it at as the greatest Rugby World Cup match ever.

A call to arms: Émile Ntamack about to celebrate the kneeling Richard Dourthe's try at Twickenham, while New Zealand's Tana Umanga looks away.

(Press Association)

42 BOD ALMIGHTY

Australia 13   British and Irish Lions 29

(The Gabba, Brisbane, June 30, 2001)

Brian O'Driscoll was one of the finest players of any generation.

In a career spanning nearly two decades there were so many highlights in the navy blue of Leinster, the green of Ireland and the red of the British and Irish Lions. He blazed onto the international scene scoring a hat-trick of tries against France at the Stade de France in 2000. It was Ireland's first win in Paris in 28 years and was, according to Irish skipper Keith Wood, the finest Irish performance of all time.

I once fancied myself as a centre, so the best of them have left a lasting impression on me. Apparently Bleddyn Williams, Jack Matthews and Jeff Butterfield deserved all the accolades but I never actually got to see them in action as I was wearing short trousers at Gwaun-cae-gurwen Primary School at the time. Cyril Davies, John Gainsford and Ian MacRae were formidable players in the 1960s whilst I was privileged to have played with and against three greats in John Dawes, Jo Maso and Mike Gibson. Others who impressed me after my retirement were Danie Gerber, Philippe Sella, Jeremy Guscott, and Tim Horan, but genetics constructed a rare model indeed in 1979 when Brian O'Driscoll came forth into the world in north Dublin.

What was so special about Brian, then? First and foremost he was a balanced runner. What's more, he had conjurer's hands, offloading in a variety of dextrous and implausible ways. Teams deliberately set out to stop him in his tracks but many found that they were unable to make contact with the swerving flyer as he accelerated away, scything and occasionally vaulting prostrate opponents. Defensively he was a Celtic warrior, his bone-crunching tackles as devastating and brave as his attacking runs. All in all, his skillset, never-say-die spirit and total commitment meant that the vast majority of his peers hated playing against him.

Give and take: Brian O'Driscoll's deft hands are too quick for Australia's James O'Connor during the second Lions Test in 2013.

(Press Association)

Brian O'Driscoll, one of the finest players of any generation, has spotted a gap against South Africa during the first Test of the 2009 Lions series. Four years earlier, he had been the Lions captain in New Zealand, before a controversial challenge brought his tour to an unceremonious end after 90 seconds of the first Test.

(Press Association)

A Brian O'Driscoll CV would have impressed rugby coaches the world over: 141 Test matches, 133 for Ireland (83 as captain, including Grand Slam season 2009); 46 international tries (the highest scoring centre of all time); British and Irish Lion on four successive tours (captain in 2005); Heineken Cup winner with Leinster (2009, 2011, 2012).

One of my favourite 'BOD' moments was at the Gabba, Brisbane, in 2001 when Australia were ripped apart by a sensational run from the Lions superstar from near his own 10-metre line. Whatever the coaches had prepared on the training ground, whatever had been preplanned – he ignored it all and went flying through the tiniest of gaps between Jeremy Paul and Daniel Herbert before beating Matt Burke with a delicate step, accelerating towards the posts with Joe Roff in his wake. A truly magnificent try.

O'Driscoll ripping Australia apart on his way to a truly magnificent try during the opening Test of the 2001 Lions series. Those trying to catch him (or just looking on in admiration) are (from the left): George Smith (7), Daniel Herbert (12), Tom Smith, Jonny Wilkinson, Glen Panaho and John Eules. (Press Association)

A very special moment for Martin Johnson as he lifts the William Webb Ellis trophy at the Telstra Stadium in Sydney in 2003.

(Press Association)

43 RUGBY WORLD CUP FINAL 2003

Australia 17   England 20   (Telstra Stadium, Sydney, November 22, 2003)

Clive Woodward's preparations before the Rugby World Cup 2003 were meticulous. The coach wanted to convince his England squad that they were good enough to beat the best in the world. He therefore persuaded the RFU at Twickenham to arrange fixtures against the might of the rugby world before the main event in Australia.

2002 was an autumn of some distinction for England with three home victories against formidable Southern Hemisphere opponents, whilst the 2003 Six Nations Championship resulted in a 12th Grand Slam for Martin Johnson's men. The rest of the world began to take note of England's achievements even more so when they travelled to Australasia in June and defeated Australia 25–14 at the Colonial Stadium in Melbourne and New Zealand 15–13 at windy Wellington. For ten minutes against the All Blacks they were down to thirteen

Jason Robinson, 'Billy Whizz', blazing past Wendell Sailor (left) and Matt Rogers on his way to England's try at the 2003 Rugby World Cup final. (Press Association)

*Now the Waugh is over! Jonny Wilkinson's
world-cup winning drop goal on it way over
Phil Waugh's head and between the uprights.*
(Press Association)

men and somehow managed to defend an all-out onslaught from the home side. It was obvious to most observers that England in 2003 had developed a killer instinct and when they trooped off the field at the Westpac Stadium the red rose army were all convinced that the Webb Ellis trophy was within their grasp.

Woodward was well aware by now that his men had the collective skills, ability and attitude to beat the best in the world. Rugby is a team game, every player must contribute but key individuals are paramount to a team's success. And in Jonny Wilkinson at fly-half England had a trump card. He was at his best during the tournament and especially so in the final where he ensured his team played in the right areas of the field. Allied to his attacking instincts, Jonny was also a fearless defender and like other class outside halves before him was comfortable off either foot. He was also a points-scoring phenomenon, universally regarded as one of the most accurate goal-kickers of all time.

Looking at their record over the previous four years England were clear favourites to win the competition but Australia had other ideas and proved that they were not going to roll over. They started promisingly – Lote Tuqiri outjumping Jason Robinson, claiming the ball in mid-air before plunging over for a try. Three Jonny Wilkinson penalties gave England a cushion before they extended their lead with a quite superb try. Dawson and Dallaglio set it up linking with the ever available Wilkinson who threw a sublime long pass towards Jason Robinson who sprinted in for the try. At half-time it was 14–5 to England.

With the England pack beginning to dominate it was rather surprising that it was Australia and Elton Flatley who claimed the second half points with Flatley's third penalty two minutes before the final whistle taking the game into extra time. Wilkinson and Flatley exchanged penalties during this nerve-racking period, but with the clock ticking towards the game's final conclusion, it was going to take something special to tip the balance.

When the oval ball left Wilkinson's trusted right foot, the words 'World Cup Winners' were written all over it. Ater 100 minutes of non-stop, combative rugby, it was a drop goal 26 seconds from the end of extra-time which propelled England and their supporters into sporting ecstasy. It elevated the players into the realms of superheroes – coach Clive Woodward became Sir Clive, outside half Jonny Wilkinson became simply Jonny and the country from Cornwall to Cumbria celebrated long into the night.

Class will always come to the fore, and Jonny is a classic example.

Main men: Lawrence Dallaglio (left) and coach Clive Woodward share the ultimate prize in rugby union.

(Press Association)

A superstar in every sense, New Zealand fly-half Dan Carter. He would need to be an escapologist, however, to wriggle free of Lions tacklers Simon Easterby (bottom) and Jason Robinson in this collision during the second Test at the Westpac Stadium in Wellington in 2005

(Press Association)

44 THE LIONS IN DANIEL'S DEN

New Zealand 48   British and Irish Lions 18

(Westpac Stadium, Wellington, July 2, 2005)

In rugby, as in all other sports, each generation produces a new superstar. This has been the case ever since William Webb Ellis first handled the ball back in the early 19th century. In the Noughties of this century the name on everyone's lips was that of Daniel Carter, the New Zealand outside half.

Carter's first international appearance was at centre against Wales at Hamilton in 2003. New Zealand won comfortably by 55–3 with the new recruit contributing 20 points. That night he made an impression on us all. There was something special about this young man: great hands, great feet and great vision allowed him to create opportunities when there appeared to be nothing on.

Unfortunately for him, and for the rest of the rugby world, Carter was absent due to injury from the final stages of the Rugby World Cups of 2007 in France and 2011 in New Zealand. But before, between and since those two competitions, he proved himself the best in the world in rugby's most iconic position.

From such a glittering career it is nigh on impossible to pick out only one gem of genius. For me, however, I think that moment came in Wellington in 2005 in the second Test between the All Blacks and the British and Irish Lions. Having lost the first Test 21–3, the Lions coach Clive Woodward was under huge pressure to manufacture a win. Before the touring party left Britain and Ireland, Woodward had predicted a series win for the Lions; after all this was the best prepared squad and the best backroom staff to have left these shores. But the manager's job was now on the line. He decided to make eleven changes (four positional) in order to ensure that his team competed manfully against the mighty All Blacks: 'When you play poorly you've got to do something. We've got to put out an attacking team because we've got to win… If you take the pats, then you've got to take the bullets'.

History will recall that this ploy did not work and the visitors lost 48–18. It was not the fact that the Lions lost but the way New Zealand played that day – it will go down as a master class in rugby football. And at the centre of it all was Daniel Carter. He scored two of his team's five tries and ended with a personal tally of 33 points.

There were times during the match (I was sitting amongst the greats of New Zealand rugby) when I felt a little embarrassed at the way the Lions were being torn apart. But then there comes a point when you have to relax and appreciate the skills on display. The move, started by Carter and ending in a try for Tana Umaga, was just one example of the genius of the man. He was the architect of each phase of play, able to create space for his fellow players and himself almost at whim. His first try was a treat, a sprint down the blind side towards the advancing Josh Lewsey and then without breaking stride or sweat a glorious kick along the ground before gathering and scoring. Easy!

At the end of the game we were all on our feet in appreciation and admiration. That night all the talk was of Daniel Carter. I had just witnessed a truly great display by an outside half. Daniel Carter, a superstar in every sense.

'Easy!' Dan Carter prepares to land for his second try of the evening, as Lions Shane Williams and Donncha O'Callaghan (right) arrive too late.

(Press Association)

45 ENDO TO END STUFF

Wales 72   Japan 18   (Millennium Stadium, Cardiff, September 20, 2007)

The scoreline is irrelevant. Yes, Wales may well have thrashed Japan in the 2007 Rugby World Cup, running in 11 tries in the process. But one Japanese try that evening was worth all the rest, a length-of-the-field effort which brought the 43,000 crowd at Cardiff to its feet.

The Cherry Blossoms were coached that year by former New Zealand Rugby World Cup winner John Kirwan, and 18 minutes into the first half his team did him proud. Wales were ahead 7–3 and mounting an attack within a metre of the Japan try line. However, the ball was dislodged and in a flash lock Hitoshi Ono had pounced and set off on a run. In support was the New Zealand-born Bryce Robins. With the Welsh defence in disarray, Robins linked with centre Shotaro Onishi, who in turn found Yuta Imamura on his shoulder. He ran in an arc, before straightening his course and delivering a perfect pass to right wing Kosuke Endo who sprinted to the try line. The move had started 100 metres back down the field and had been a text-book display of how to give and take the ball at speed. It even reminded the oldies present of the try scored by Tadayuki Itoh when Japan paid their first ever visit to Wales in 1973.

I also went on our first ever tour of Japan in 1975, where games were played at Osaka and at Tokyo's National Stadium. Although played in blistering heat, a situation we were not accustomed to, Wales won both matches by a comfortable margin. The welcome we received from the Japanese people was as warm and courteous as we had experienced anywhere on tour.

On one of our days off J.P.R. Williams and I had been invited to take part in a tennis match with two of the country's up-and-coming players. We narrowly lost the first set and I remember thinking that this was not altogether a bad thing: our hosts wouldn't have appreciated losing face, after all. However, during the next drinks break, JPR took me to one side and whispered in my ear, 'Either you take this seriously, Gareth, or I'm walking off.' We went on to win the next two sets with ease. Never doubt that JPR is nothing if not competitive!

Kosuke Endo, scorer of a spectacular Japanese try at Cardiff in 2007.

(Press Association)

He mesmerised and entertained: Wales's Shane Williams, in action for the Lions during the third Test of their 2009 series in South Africa.

(Press Association)

46 SHANE

South Africa 37 Wales 21   (Loftus Versfeld, Pretoria, June 14, 2008)

You know you're a legend in Wales when your Christian name suffices. Barry. Gerald. Phil. And more recently, Shane. I rest my case.

It must be over three years now since Shane Williams retired from playing international rugby but I still find myself reminiscing about the exploits of one of the finest wings of the modern era. I can even visit YouTube and the like to remind myself of what this quiet, modest individual actually accomplished. His tally of 60 international tries (58 for Wales and 2 for the British and Irish Lions) is a truly outstanding achievement. What can you say when the likes of David Campese, John Kirwan, Gerald Davies, Michael Lynagh, Philippe Sella and Bryan Habana are genuinely excited by his performances?

When Williams had the ball in hand, the game changed: defences were rooted to the spot and then breached in the twinkling of an eye. Irrespective of his own coach's philosophy, the will-o'-the-wisp superhero from the Amman valley knew only one way: attack was always the best form of both defence and attack! And how could the opposition coach prepare a strategy to contain a player for whom the unexpected was second nature? He mesmerised and entertained: he was pure rugby box office.

A compilation of Shane's greatest tries would be an ideal birthday gift for any rugby addict. It would feature those three majestic efforts against the Pumas at Buenos Aires in 2004, not to mention his scampering in at the corner against England at Cardiff during our 2005 Grand Slam campaign. And what of his sorcery to silence the Irish at Croke Park in 2008, or, if you prefer, his gravity-and-touchline-defying score against Scotland at Cardiff that same year?

I have a personal favourite, however, one that would qualify for a top-ten place in my lifetime try ceremony award. Importantly it was one scored against quality opposition: in 2008 the Springboks were the Rugby World Cup holders, and thus the match in Pretoria was advertised as World champions against European champions, Wales having just completed their second Grand Slam in three years.

OK, Wales lost, but Shane's try just before half-time was a brilliant display of Welsh wizardry to rival the spells cast by Barry, Gerald and Phil in their time. On this occasion I was watching from the comfort of my own home, entranced as the impossible suddenly became possible.

South Africa had just lost possession near the touchline, when Shane picked up the loose ball some 40 metres from the Springbok try line, with six or seven defenders in attendance. Instinctively, he veered infield, then he changed direction and swerved back out towards the touchline. The defence seemed to be in a state of suspended animation as Shane sprinted towards the try line. Not one South African hand was laid on him throughout the entire move.

43,393 supporters stood on their feet in appreciation hailing Shane as the hero of the hour. Meanwhile, at home, I too was on my feet shouting for my wife Maureen to come and watch the action replay!

One of my top ten favourite tries, Shane Williams touches down at Pretoria in 2008, in spite of South Africa's Adrian Jacobs's try-line tackle.

(Press Association)

*'Bye, bye, Botha!' Shane Williams on his way
to that dazzling try against the Springboks,
leaving Bakkies Botha a long, long way away.*

(Press Association)

Leinster's inspirational Heineken Cup final match-winner Jonny Sexton orchestrates play for the Lions against Australia in the third Test of the 2013 series.

(Press Association)

47 SEXTON REFRESHES THE PARTS...

Leinster 33   Northampton 22   (Millennium Stadium, Cardiff, May 21, 2011)

I know that we sportsmen can't resist a good cliché, but this truly was a game of two halves! Northampton outstanding in the first half, Leinster simply sensational in the second.

Not all Heineken Cup finals since 1996 have lived up to the pre-match hype. Some have, mind: CA Brive royally entertained the crowd at Cardiff in 1997, crossing for four sparkling tries against Leicester; who can forget Austin Healey's all-round brilliance at the Parc des Princes in 2001 in Leicester's 34–30 victory over Stade Français, or Robert Howley's last-minute match-winning touchline sprint at Twickenham as Wasps took down Toulouse 27–20? However, for pure drama, the 2011 final between Northampton and Leinster was one magic moment after another.

Northampton led 22–6 at half-time thanks mainly to their set piece domination, with Phil Dowson, Ben Foden and Dylan Hartley scoring crucial tries in front of 72,456 spectators. Leinster seemed to have been demolished by Northampton: Dylan Hartley's team had the Midas touch and everyone present felt that the cup was already theirs.

Word has it that at the interval fly-half Jonny Sexton gave a rousing team talk to his fellow players in which he cited Liverpool's Champions League comeback in 2005 when the Reds came back from a 3–0 deficit to beat AC Milan via a penalty shoot-out. A fired-up Leinster emerged from the dressing room after half-time and proceeded to give the Northampton Saints a master class in how to play rugby football. It was a remarkable turnaround with Jonny Sexton at the heart of it all. What a display of fly-half play we witnessed! Even Barry John and Phil Bennett, who were watching from the press box and commentary position, could not fail to be impressed!

Within the space of ten minutes Sexton had scored two tries. The first saw him striding purposefully through a gap in the Northampton defence and then cleverly looping around the supporting Jamie Heaslip for his second. Leinster went on to score 27 unanswered points in a quite memorable second forty. Sexton deservedly claimed the man-of-the-match award not only for his match tally of 28 points but also for his leadership, inspiration and otherwordly elusiveness around the field. Following the victory, Leinster joined the list of Heineken Cup greats with two triumphs in three years.

Grand Slam winner in 2012 George North picks up speed at the Stade de France in 2015. A star of Wales's 2011 Rugby World Cup campaign, and with the Lions in Australia in 2013, North is destined for great things.

(Press Association)

48 GRAND SLAM HAT-TRICK

Wales in 2005, 2008 and 2012

Winning one Grand Slam is a remarkable feat. To win as many as three within the space of seven years is unbelieveable, but during the past 110 years, Wales have managed it on three occasions. The first was between 1908 and 1911, a golden age in Welsh rugby, which had commenced with the never-to-be-forgotten victory against the All Blacks in 1905. Although John Gwilliam in the early 1950s is the only Welsh captain to lead Wales to two Grand Slams his team failed to emulate the achievement of the pre-First World War XV.

Along with J.P.R. Williams and Gerald Davies, I was fortunate enough to have played in three Grand Slams sides, those of 1971, 1976 and 1978. Before the introduction of the Rugby World Cup in 1987, the Grand Slam was the ultimate for a player from the Northern Hemisphere. To this day I still treasure the memories and occasionally switch on our DVD player to relive some of the tries and the magic moments.

During the past 35 years I've spent time in the commentary box witnessing rugby union of the very highest quality. Wales became the laughing stock of the rugby world in the 1980s and 1990s when players left in droves to Rugby League. However, in 2005, against all expectation, Wales once again became a major player. Under the captaincy of Gareth Thomas and Michael Owen Wales surprised their most faithful fans and harshest critics by winning their first Grand Slam since 1978. What is more, it was achieved with a breath of fresh air with the team adopting an attacking formula.

The decisive match in that series was the one against France at the Stade de France. It was a classic encounter eventually won by the men in red who, after an indifferent first half, tore up the script and decided to throw caution to the wind. The comeback was instigated by Stephen Jones who, with a do-or-die counter-attack, opened up a disjointed French defence. The movement swept from one side of the field to the other resulting in a Martyn Williams try. Within minutes, the ever alert Williams was again the beneficiary after taking a quick penalty near the French line. Confidence soared and Wales went on to record a great victory.

2008 was Warren Gatland's first season in charge and his influence was immediate. However, it has to be said that Wales's results were often fashioned by individiual genius. Under Ryan Jones's captaincy Wales came back from the dead at Twickenham with Lee Byrne and Mike Phillips crossing for match-winning tries. And it was that man Shane Williams who broke Irish hearts in

Adam Jones, Grand Slam tight-head prop in 2005, 2008 and 2011.   (Press Association)

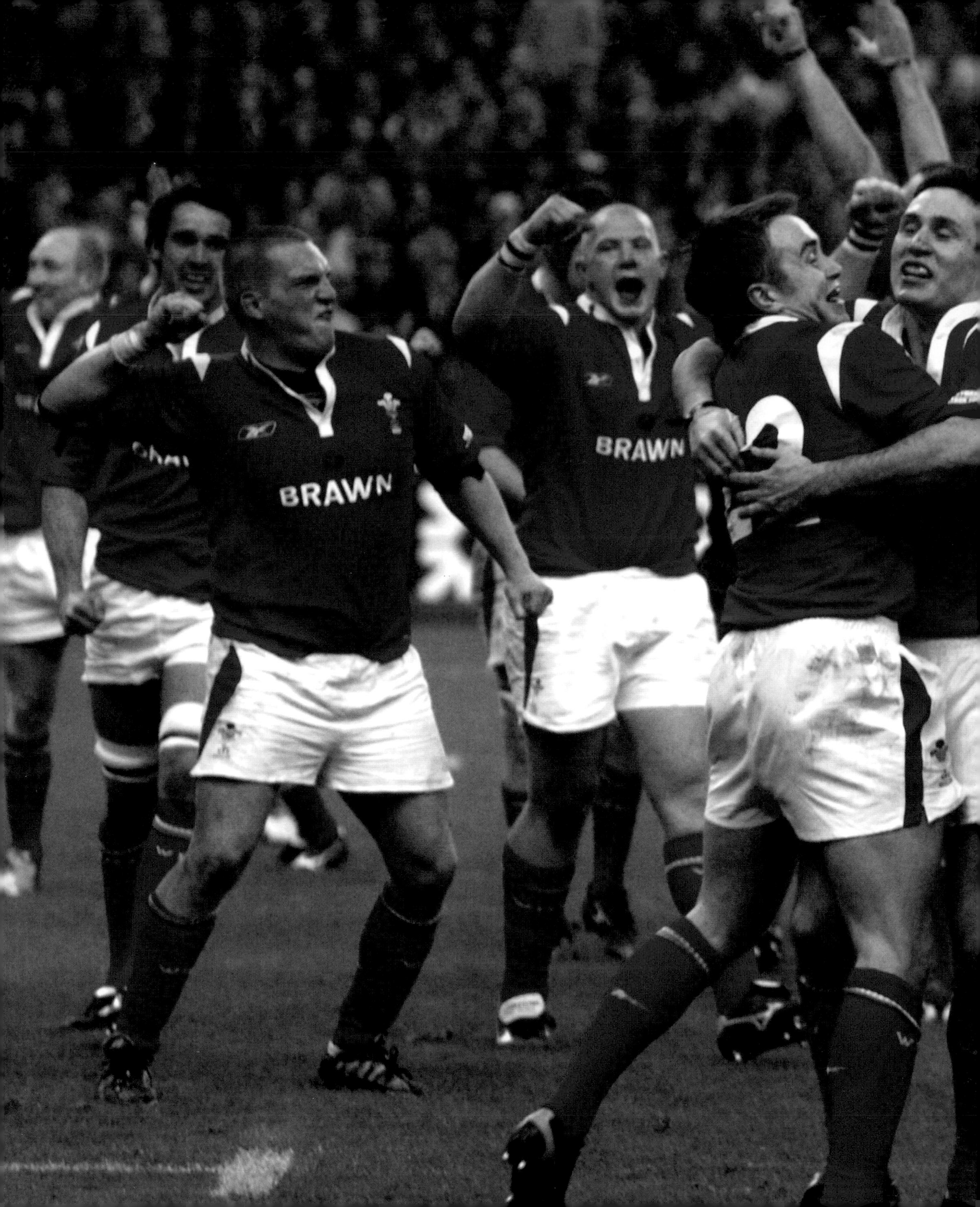
BRAWN
BRAWN

'Come on!' Wales celebrate their remarkable comeback victory in Paris in 2005: (from the left) try scorer Martyn Williams raises his arms, Jonathan Thomas smiles, Gethin Jenkins and John Yapp clench their fists, Rhys Williams and Stephen Jones hug, and full-back Kevin Morgan jumps for joy. Meanwhile, behind them, Robin McBryde (16) ties his laces!

(Press Association)

Ryan Jones dives over to score against Scotland in 2005, much to scrum-half Dwayne Peel's delight. Jones is another to have figured in all three Grand Slams, and was captain in 2008.

(Press Association)

Dublin squeezing over in the corner at Croke Park to claim the only try in an intriguing contest.

It became three Grand Slams in eight seasons in 2012 when Sam Warburton, along with Gethin Jenkins, led Wales to their eleventh title. The match againt England at Twickenham was a pivotal one. When all seemed lost super-sub Scott Williams wrestled the ball free at a maul and ran fully 30 metres unopposed for an opportunist try. During the campaign Leigh Halfpenny, tutored by Neil Jenkins, proved a lethal goal-kicker from short and long distances.

Three Slam successes in less than a decade is indeed a remarkable achievement, only bettered by England and France, as it happens. England recorded four Grand Slams between 1921 and 1928 and three between 1991 and 1995, whilst France won four Grand Slams in eight seasons between 1997 and 2004.

Two-time Grand Slam scrum-half Mike Phillips tries to shake off Irish opposite number Eoin Reddan at Croke Park in 2008, when Wales won 16–12. Grimacing in support is Ian Gough, whilst the two nearest Irishmen are Andrew Trimble (11) and Jamie Heaslip. (Press Association)

Jonathan Davies beats Gordon D'Arcy single-handed at the Aviva Stadium in Dublin, as Wales win 23–21, taking their first step towards the 2012 Grand Slam. Davies scored two tries, George North (with finger raised) one, whilst Leigh Halfpenny's boot did the rest.

(Press Association)

*Two skippers head to head:
South Africa's Jean de Villiers (left)
knows only one way against New
Zealand's Richie McCaw during the epic
encounter at Ellis Park in 2013.*

(Press Association)

49 QUICK DRAW McCAW AND MR GYM SHOES

South Africa 27   New Zealand 38   (Ellis Park, Johannesburg, October 5, 2013)

It was the afternoon when two great Southern Hemisphere teams clashed – South Africa, Rugby World Cup winners 2007, welcomed New Zealand, Rugby World Cup winners 2011, to Ellis Park. It was also the afternoon when two of the game's icons came face to face – South African speedster Bryan Habana and inspirational All Blacks leader Richie McCaw. New Zealand's record at Ellis Park was indifferent with only three victories (1928, 1992 and 1997) in eleven attempts. However, the All Blacks had dominated the Tri Nations (renamed The Rugby Championship in 2012) winning the competition on 11 occasions since its inception in 1996.

Although the All Blacks were on an unbeaten run of nine matches, it had been a promising season for Jean de Villiers' Springboks. They realised that a bonus point win would see them claim the title for the first time since 2009. In all honesty no team should have lived with South Africa when playing at altitude but the All Blacks as usual had come prepared and had acclimatised accordingly. It was a match which was later described as one of the most exciting ever played between the two countries with the lead changing hands on eight occasions.

Kieran Read's miraculous out-of-the-back-door off-load created the first of the game's nine tries allowing Ben Smith to veer inside and race in for the score. However, the Springboks retaliated immediately with two outstanding tries by Habana. Former All Black scrum-half and current pundit Justin Marshall calls the great Springbok wing 'Mr Gym Shoes' and his blistering speed left several All Blacks trailing in his wake. The first was created by Vermeulen's clinical break and superb long pass, whilst the second resulted from a remarkable off-load in the tackle from Willem Alberts. Habana's kick and chase was typical of the man and he raced in to score. South Africa were on fire!

New Zealand were down but far from out. As on so many occasions in the past, the All Blacks responded to skipper McCaw. He was at the heart of everything, constantly leading by example, encouraging his players to give their all to the cause – and how they responded! Liam Messam was the first to rise to the challenge crossing for two tries just before half-time, helped over by team-mate Brodie Retallick for the first and then in a perfect position to finish

Mr Gym Shoes', Bryan Habana, pictured here with the Rugby World Cup trophy in 2007.

(Press Association)

Le Roux on le roll: livewire South African full-back Willie le Roux beats Dane Coles's tackle to score one of his side's four tries.

(Press Association)

New Zealand's Kieran Read, the IRB's world player of the year in 2013, pursues the same loose ball as Bryan Habana, whilst Jean de Villiers is still in his blocks.

(Press Association)

off a superb movement involving Cruden, Read, Smith and Savea for his second. The All Blacks were revitalised and were leading 21–15 at the interval. Such was the attacking spectacle that I was glued to the television set at home.

Amazingly, both teams emerged for the second half with similar intentions. It was a non-stop, one-hundred-miles-an-hour contest and South Africa retaliated immediately with two tries from Le Roux and skipper de Villiers. New Zealand were trailing 27–24 going into the final quarter and looked in trouble when Messam and Franks were both issued with yellow cards by referee Nigel Owens. With the All Blacks down to 14 men, McCaw exhibited superhuman leadership qualities on the field. His fellow players reciprocated with two late scores – replacement Beauden Barrett sliced the Springboks apart for the fourth try before McCaw's perfectly timed pass created a fifth and final try for Kieran Read. It was game, set and match to the All Blacks who claimed their twelfth Rugby Championshp title.

Ben Smith opens the scoring for the All Blacks on what proved a rollercoaster evening for all involved. (Press Association)

An uplifting moment! Stade Francais' Sergio Parisse, seen here outleaping Clermont during the Top 14 final in 2015, produced a miraculous rugby moment in the semi-final against Toulon.   (Press Association)

50   MIRACLE AT BORDEAUX

Stade Français 33   Toulon 16   (Stade de Bordeaux, Friday, June 5, 2015)

It was an early morning text message from my son Rhys:

> Weles ti'r gêm nithwr? A weles ti bas Parisse? Ma'r cwbwl 'da fi ar Skyplus.
> Galwa.
> (Did you see last night's match? Did you see Parisse's pass? It's all on
> Skyplus. Call me.)

Over the last 12 years I have been a great admirer of Sergio Parisse. The Italian
No. 8 born in La Plata, Argentina to Italian parents, joined Stade Français
from Treviso in 2005. By June 2015 he had won a total of 112 Italian caps for
Italy – the first as a raw 18-year-old against New Zealand in Hamilton in 2004.
From my own experiences I know how difficult it is for players to impress
under pressure but Parisse has always had that ability of producing five-star
performances when the going gets tough.

I did call in at Rhys's house and together we watched his brief recording of
the Top 14 semi-final between Parisse's Stade Français and Toulon.

Toulon had started positively and after 23 minutes were leading 10–6
when Stade Français forced a turnover in midfield inside the Toulon 22.
Half-backs Dupuy and Steyn took advantage of the situation, moving the ball
swiftly towards the near touchline where prop forward Rabah Slimani gave
a flat pass to Sergio Parisse. The No. 8 quickly realised that there was very
little chance of him reaching the try line and, with Bryan Habana and hooker
Guilhem Guirado in the act of hauling him to ground, he was left with just one
alternative. Signor Parisse produced what can only be described as a moment
of magic, a quite miraculous pass. I asked Rhys to replay the movement again,
and again, and again to confirm that what I'd seen with my own eyes had
actually happened!

Sergio, who was skirting the touchline, held the ball in his right hand
and delivered the final coup de grâce. He slid the ball behind his back and
in an intricate reverse movement directed a pass into the waiting hands of
flanker Raphael Lakafia who crossed unopposed. All the money in Monsieur
Boudjellal's coffers could not have bought such a moment of pure genius and
Stade went on to win the match.

Acknowledgements

I was born and bred in a patch of land where the upper Amman valley and upper Swansea valley converge. As a result of the area's complex boundary lines I received my early secondary education at Pontardawe Grammar Technical School in the Swansea valley.

My home village of Gwaun-cae-gurwen, along with its neighbouring villages, is steeped in rugby history with approximately 24 players having represented Wales since 1881. The area can also boast a quite remarkable statistic – five Lions (R.H. Williams, Clem Thomas, Trevor Evans, Shane Williams and I) were born and bred within three miles of Cresci's Ice Cream Parlour in Gwaun-cae-gurwen! And, of course, Clive Rowlands from nearby Cwmtwrch was the Lions' manager in Australia in 1989.

When Wales defeated the All Blacks in 1935, the Welsh captain was none other than the great Claude Davey who spent his childhood years on Leyshon Road in Gwaun-cae-gurwen. My father constantly reminded me that Emrys Evans, who lived in a neighbouring steeet, was quite unique. He was selected to play for Wales as a prop forward against England at Twickenham in 1937 and then chosen as a back-row forward against Scotland and Ireland in 1939. My brother Gethin brings me back down to earth when I return home, 'Remember Gar, you're not the first player from Gwaun-cae-gurwen to score a try for Wales against the Springboks. Will 'Skeely' Davies plunged over the try line on his debut at St Helen's in 1931!' However, I feel honoured and privileged to have represented my home village on the international stage and would like to thank its inhabitants for supporting me throughout my playing days.

I also have to pay tribute to the late Bill Samuel for the part he played in my development as a sportsman. Similarly I'm also indebted to the late Jack Hamer whose patience and unstinting support proved crucial at a time when life was often difficult for a young amateur rugby player. I'd also like to thank friends and family who have been supportive of me in so many areas of my life over the years, especially my wife Maureen, Owen and Rhian, Rhys and Eirlys, along with my grandchildren Ela, Dylan, Tomi and Harri.

I would also like to take this opportunity of thanking Gomer Press in Llandysul and in particular Ceri Wyn Jones for his guidance and enthusiasm in formulating the publication, whilst my colleague Alun Wyn Bevan deserves credit for his encouragement, prompting and word-processing skills. He keeps on reminding me that he once refereed a Cardiff vs Pontypridd Boxing Day match at the Arms Park when I apparently scored a try from 70 metres out. According to Alun, it was a great rugby moment – but it hasn't made the cut this time! If your classic great rugby moment hasn't been included here, it may well appear in the next edition!